T0220594

PHP CLI

Create Command Line Interface Scripts with PHP

Rob Aley

Apress®

PHP CLI: Create Command Line Interface Scripts with PHP

Rob Aley
Oxford, United Kingdom

ISBN-13 (pbk): 978-1-4842-2237-9   ISBN-13 (electronic): 978-1-4842-2238-6
DOI 10.1007/978-1-4842-2238-6

Library of Congress Control Number: 2016951308

Copyright © 2016 by Rob Aley

This work is subject to copyright. All rights are reserved by the Publisher, whether the whole or part of the material is concerned, specifically the rights of translation, reprinting, reuse of illustrations, recitation, broadcasting, reproduction on microfilms or in any other physical way, and transmission or information storage and retrieval, electronic adaptation, computer software, or by similar or dissimilar methodology now known or hereafter developed.

Trademarked names, logos, and images may appear in this book. Rather than use a trademark symbol with every occurrence of a trademarked name, logo, or image we use the names, logos, and images only in an editorial fashion and to the benefit of the trademark owner, with no intention of infringement of the trademark.

The use in this publication of trade names, trademarks, service marks, and similar terms, even if they are not identified as such, is not to be taken as an expression of opinion as to whether or not they are subject to proprietary rights.

While the advice and information in this book are believed to be true and accurate at the date of publication, neither the authors nor the editors nor the publisher can accept any legal responsibility for any errors or omissions that may be made. The publisher makes no warranty, express or implied, with respect to the material contained herein.

Managing Director: Welmoed Spahr
Lead Editor: Steve Anglin
Technical Reviewer: Tri Phan
Editorial Board: Steve Anglin, Pramila Balan, Laura Berendson, Aaron Black, Louise Corrigan, Jonathan Gennick, Robert Hutchinson, Celestin Suresh John, Nikhil Karkal, James Markham, Susan McDermott, Matthew Moodie, Natalie Pao, Gwenan Spearing
Coordinating Editor: Mark Powers
Copy Editor: Kim Wimpsett
Compositor: SPi Global
Indexer: SPi Global
Artist: SPi Global
Cover image designed by Freepik

Distributed to the book trade worldwide by Springer Science+Business Media New York, 233 Spring Street, 6th Floor, New York, NY 10013. Phone 1-800-SPRINGER, fax (201) 348-4505, e-mail orders-ny@springer-sbm.com, or visit www.springeronline.com. Apress Media, LLC is a California LLC and the sole member (owner) is Springer Science + Business Media Finance Inc (SSBM Finance Inc). SSBM Finance Inc is a **Delaware** corporation.

For information on translations, please e-mail rights@apress.com, or visit www.apress.com.

Apress and friends of ED books may be purchased in bulk for academic, corporate, or promotional use. eBook versions and licenses are also available for most titles. For more information, reference our Special Bulk Sales–eBook Licensing web page at www.apress.com/bulk-sales.

Any source code or other supplementary materials referenced by the author in this text are available to readers at www.apress.com/9781484222379. For detailed information about how to locate your book's source code, go to www.apress.com/source-code/. Readers can also access source code at SpringerLink in the Supplementary Material section for each chapter.

Printed on acid-free paper

Contents at a Glance

About the Author ix

About the Technical Reviewer xi

Acknowledgments xiii

■Chapter 1: Introduction 1

■Chapter 2: An Overview of CLI Programming in PHP..................... 7

■Chapter 3: Understanding and Using the CLI SAPI 13

■Chapter 4: User-Facing Software.................................... 31

■Chapter 5: PHP CLI Scripts and Your System 41

■Chapter 6: Where to Now? (Or, Thanks and Feedback) 45

■Appendix A: Compiling and Installing PHP, Extensions, and Libs....... 47

■Appendix B: Sources of Help 57

Index... 61

Contents

About the Author ix

About the Technical Reviewer xi

Acknowledgments xiii

■Chapter 1: Introduction 1

"Use PHP? We're Not Building a Website, You Know!" 1

Are You New to PHP? 2

Reader Prerequisites 3

An Important Note About Operating Systems 3

About the Sample Code 4

External Resources 4

PHP 7 5

■Chapter 2: An Overview of CLI Programming in PHP 7

Getting Away from the Web 7

PHP Without a Web Server 7

PHP Versions: What's Yours? 8

A Few Good Reasons *Not* to Do It in PHP 9

High-Performance Requirements 9

Don't (Necessarily) Re-invent the Wheel 9

Keeping the Source Closed 9

Thinking About Security 10

CLI-Specific Code Frameworks 12

■**Chapter 3: Understanding and Using the CLI SAPI** **13**

What's Different About the CLI SAPI? 13

CLI SAPI Installation 14

PHP Command-Line Options 15

Command-Line Arguments for Your Script 20

The Many Ways to Call PHP Scripts 21

From a File 21

From a String 22

From STDIN 22

As a Self-executing Script: Unix/Linux 23

As a Self-executing Script: Windows 25

Windows php-win.exe 25

Quitting Your Script 26

PHP REPLs 27

■**Chapter 4: User-Facing Software** **31**

Command-Line Interface Basics 31

Advanced Command-Line Input 35

Using STDIN, STOUT, and STDERR 38

CLI Helper Libraries 40

■**Chapter 5: PHP CLI Scripts and Your System** **41**

Starting External Processes from PHP, or "Shelling Out" 41

File Status and Realpath Caches 42

APC and Other Code Caches 44

■**Chapter 6: Where to Now? (Or, Thanks and Feedback)** **45**

Giving Feedback and Getting Help and Support 45

■**Appendix A: Compiling and Installing PHP, Extensions, and Libs......47**

Compiling and Installing PHP 48

    Windows 48

    OS X 48

    Linux/Unix 49

Compiling and Installing (Extra) Core Extensions 51

Installing Multiple Versions of PHP 52

PEAR and PECL 53

Composer 54

Symfony2 Bundles 55

■**Appendix B: Sources of Help 57**

The PHP Manual 57

Official Mailing Lists 57

Stack Overflow 58

Other Books 58

Newsgroups 58

PHP Subredit 58

PHP on GitHub 59

PHP News Sites 59

Index.. 61

About the Author

Rob Aley I've been programming in PHP since late 2000. Initially it wasn't by choice because my preferred languages at the time were Perl and Delphi (also known as Object Pascal). Things began to change after I graduated from the University of Leeds with a degree in computer science in 1999 and started out in a career as a freelance web developer. After only a couple of months I was offered the opportunity to take over a (relatively speaking) substantial government website contract from a friend who was exiting the freelance world for the safer and saner world of full-time employment. The only catch was that several thousand lines of code had already been written, and they were written in a relatively new language called PHP. Oh, and the only other catch was that I had about a week to learn it before taking over the site. So, as was the way at the time, I popped down to the local Waterstones bookshop. (For the younger among you that's where we used to get books. And we had to go out and get them. Or order online and wait days for them to be delivered.) With my paper copy of *The Generic Beginner's Complete Guide to PHP and MySQL for Dummies Compendium* in hand (I may not have recalled the title completely correctly), I settled down with a pint of ale (I'm in Yorkshire at this point, remember) and set about reading it. A few days later I was coding like a pro (well, stuff was working), and 12 years later I haven't looked back. After a varied career as a freelancer and starting up a couple of, er, startups (IT related and not) with varying (usually dismal) success, I spent the past ten years as a full-time programmer at the University of Oxford. My day job involved performing medium-scale data acquisition and management, doing statistical analysis, and providing user interfaces for researchers and the public. The majority of my development work was done in PHP, either developing new projects or gluing together other people's software, systems, and databases. I've recently left the university to concentrate on writing books like this and providing consulting and training (in PHP, information governance, and related areas). But I'm still programming in PHP!

Throughout my career I've always used PHP for web development, but for desktop GUI work I initially used Delphi (and then Free-Pascal/Lazarus), complemented with bash shell scripting for other tasks. This was mainly because I learned them while at university. However, as PHP has matured, I've increasingly used it beyond the Web, and now I rarely use anything else for any programming or scripting task I encounter. Having been immersed in other languages such as C++, JavaScript, Fortran, and Lisp (and probably others that my brain has chosen deliberately not to remember) by necessity during university and in some of my freelance jobs, I can honestly say that PHP is now my language of choice, rather than of necessity.

When I'm not tied to a computer, I would like to say I have lots of varied and interesting hobbies. I used to have. I could write a whole book (which wouldn't sell well) about where I've been and what I've done, and I'd like to think it's made me a well-rounded person. But these days I don't have any. In large part this is because of the demands of my three gorgeous young daughters, Ellie, Izzy, and Indy; my gorgeous wife, Parv; and my even more gorgeous cat, Mia. And I wouldn't have it any other way. That's what I tell myself, anyway.

About the Technical Reviewer

Tri Phan is the founder of the Programming Learning Channel on YouTube. He has almost a decade of experience in the software industry. Specifically, he has worked for many outsourcing companies and has written applications in a variety of programming languages such as PHP, Java, and C#. In addition, he has more than six years of experience in teaching at international and technological centers such as Aptech, NIIT, and Kent College.

Acknowledgments

Isaac Newton said, "If I have seen further, it is by standing on the shoulders of giants." This book builds on, and I hope adds to, the work of many others, the most notable of whom I would like to acknowledge here.

- *The authors of, and contributors to, the official PHP manual*: An invaluable reference for PHP functions and syntax, to which I referred frequently during writing this book, both for fact checking and as an aide-memoir. Thanks!

- *The collective PHP wisdom of the Internet*: For more than 12 years I've used you for learning, research, play, and profit. Too many sites and too many people to list here; if you've written about PHP on the Web, then you may well be one of them. Thanks!

- *My family*: For allowing me a modicum of time to write this book and supporting me unconditionally in everything I do. Usually. If I ask first. And there's not something more important going on. And usually with conditions. Thanks!

CHAPTER 1

Introduction

"Use PHP? We're Not Building a Website, You Know!"

Both its current recursive moniker (PHP: PHP HyperText Preprocessor) and the name originally bestowed upon it by its creator Rasmus Lerdorf (PHP: Personal Home Page) reinforce the widely held view that PHP is a scripting language for the Web. And that was true back in 1995 when PHP was first created and for a number of years afterward. In the web arena, PHP excels. It's easy to use, quick to develop in, widely deployed, and tightly integrated into web stacks (it's usually the *P* in LAMP, WAMP, MAMP, and so on), and of course it is free and open source.

But many people don't realize (or haven't noticed or choose not to notice) that PHP has evolved. It now closely resembles a modern, general-purpose programming language. This lack of recognition is partly PHP's own fault because it took a long time to get some of the fundamentals in place, such as object-oriented programming (OOP) language constructs and even the ability to run at all without a web server being involved. Further, the programming community hasn't helped; many programmers had a hard time seeing the potential for PHP to bring its rapid dynamic development model out of the Web and into the wider computing environment, and many simply stuck with the "web scripting for beginners" dogma that was only really true of its early years.

Recent releases in particular have brought mainstream language features (for example, closures, traits, better language support, namespaces, and late static binding among many others) to the table. Performance has jumped up and up and up, memory usage (a bugbear of older versions) has dropped considerably, and PHP is now one of the leaner popular scripting languages. For even higher-performance needs, PHP 7 has dramatically rewritten the Zend Engine (giving up to twice the performance of 5.6), and Facebook (the biggest user of PHP around) is one of several companies releasing alternative interpreters/virtual machines (VMs), leading to performance increases of up to six times that achievable with the old Zend Engine. The recent release of PHP 7 and the upswing in community involvement are indicative that reports of PHP's demise are quite premature!

© Rob Aley 2016
R. Aley, *PHP CLI*, DOI 10.1007/978-1-4842-2238-6_1

But why, why, oh, why create command-line scripts in PHP? Why not whip up a bash shell script? Why not learn C++ or another language typically used for software projects? The truth is these are valid options, and life may well work out just fine for you. But why turn down the opportunity to use your existing skills? Why not use PHP's integrated database access, reuse existing code and data from your web projects, take advantage of PHP's easy-to-use network libraries and functions, wallow in flexible text and data handling, and mix shell commands and other languages into PHP as needed to get best of both worlds? In short, why the heck not?

Ideally I've sold you on the story that PHP is a cross-platform, rapid-development-focused, versatile language and is ideal for many different types of software. The aim of this book is to give you, the PHP coder, an insight into one specific type of software: using PHP to build command-line tools that live beyond the Web. I'll show you the essential ingredients needed to transform your existing web-based PHP skills to the command line so you can get up and running as quickly as possible with the tools you already know.

Further Reading

- "PHP is much better than you think": An article by Fabien Pontencier outlining the positives of PHP development and talking about the changes in the PHP ecosystem

    - http://fabien.potencier.org/article/64/php-is-much-better-than-you-think

Are You New to PHP?

This book shows PHP developers how they can use their existing skills to write CLI software instead of web pages. However, I appreciate that some readers may be new to PHP and are reading this book to get a feel for what PHP is capable of. If you're already a programmer, albeit not well versed in PHP, the comprehensive official PHP manual may be the best place to begin to get a feel for the differences between PHP and the languages you are used to using.

If you're not already a programmer, there are numerous "beginning PHP" books available from your favorite e-book retailer. In either case, the wider Web also provides its usual breadth of in-depth knowledge and tutorials, just a judicious Google search away.

Finally, newcomer or experienced programmer, if you're thinking of getting serious about PHP, it may be worth taking a look at some PHP "best practice" websites before diving headlong into coding. It may save you a lot of trouble in the long run.

Further Reading

- The official PHP manual

    - http://www.php.net/manual

- A free online PHP course for beginners

    - http://ureddit.com/class/55471/programming-in-php

- "PHP: The Right Way": A quick reference for PHP best practices, accepted coding standards, and links to authoritative tutorials

    - http://www.phptherightway.com/

- "PHP Best Practices": A short, practical guide for common and confusing PHP tasks

    - http://phpbestpractices.org/

- "PHP Study Guide": A PHP study guide aimed at those wanting to pass the Zend Certified Engineer (ZCE) exam

    - http://php-guide.evercodelab.com/

- "Zend Certification Preparation Pack": Sample questions and answers plus a guide to preparing and taking the ZCE exam

    - https://leanpub.com/zce

- "PSR-What?": A guide to the PHP Standards Recommendations (PSRs)

    - http://www.lornajane.net/posts/2013/psr-what

Reader Prerequisites

To make the most of this book, you should have basic experience of programming in PHP (most likely for the Web), a general programming or IT background, and a willingness to learn and be taken outside of your comfort zone.

This book isn't an introduction to PHP or programming in general. Although you don't need a computing degree or knowledge of advanced programming concepts, the book is aimed at the level of an average PHP programmer (one who has explored more than the basics of PHP) and tries to explain any necessary concepts as we go along. It is also useful for advanced programmers who may choose to use it as a quick reference for exploring the PHP CLI features.

An Important Note About Operating Systems

PHP runs on many operating systems, including Linux, Microsoft Windows, and Apple OS X, and code often runs in an identical manner. However, there are, of course, differences because of the file system, operating system (OS), available libraries, and so on, but covering these all in this book would not be practical. In addition, some features such as those reliant on POSIX standards aren't (easily) available on some systems like Windows. As OS X was derived from a POSIX-compliant operating system, you will likely find more of the code compatible than with Windows, but your experience may still vary. A good source of information for OS-specific issues is the official PHP online manual and, in particular, the user comments at the bottom of each page. Where possible, areas specific to a particular OS will be covered; for instance, we will look at how to access the Windows Registry.

About the Sample Code

As you'll see throughout the book I mainly use "traditional" imperative/procedural PHP in my coding examples to keep things as simple as possible for coders of all abilities. This book isn't designed to be a lesson in coding best practices or style, a guide to OOP programming, or an endorsement of any kind of programming model or dogma. I also avoid the use of any code frameworks. Many frameworks are based around the web model and don't always perform as intended in the kind of applications I'll be covering, although some do now have "console" or "cli" modules. MVC-style frameworks can be useful when building graphical user interface (GUI) applications (indeed, the MVC paradigm predates the web considerably!), but because of the many different implementation details and styles, I'll stick to framework-less code here.

It should be clear from the plain, straightforward PHP code presented how it can be used or adapted to suit your own programming style, framework, or model. I will be mainly talking about the task-specific implementation details, leaving the hot topic of programming itself to the many other books available.

All the sample PHP source code in this book is available for you to use and do with as you please without limit or license. Use or abuse it as you see fit!

If you have trouble running or understanding the sample code, see the "Giving Feedback and Getting Help and Support" section in Chapter 6 of this book for details on how to contact me for help.

External Resources

Throughout the book I will point you in the direction of external tools, resources, and information via toolboxes and "Further Reading" lists as follows:

Toolbox	A Toolbox Like This

Toolboxes like this contain details of useful online tools and installable software.

Main documentation and installation information	`http://www.a-useful.tool/`
Main documentation and installation information	`http://wiki.a-useful.tool`

Further Reading

- Useful articles, tutorials, and reference information will be presented in "Further Reading" sections like this

  - `https://www.very-useful-info.book/`

PHP 7

The next generation of PHP, PHP 7 (don't ask what happened to 6; it's a long story), was recently released. All the code and the techniques I talk about in this book should run and operate in the same way whether you are using PHP 5 or PHP 7. When I talk about, for example, installing PHP, I'll refer to PHP 5 (for example, `sudo apt-get install php5-cli`) because that is what most people are still using at the moment. However, if your platform supports 7, then go ahead and use that instead (for example, on the latest Ubuntu version at the time of writing, 16.04, the package `php7.0-cli` is now in the standard repositories); it should all work in the same way.

If you are lucky enough to have the choice of which version to use and are planning on writing CLI scripts, here are some points to consider:

> *Speed*: The number-one thing you'll notice with 7 is the increase in speed. While successive releases of 5.*x* versions have consistently pushed speed higher (and resource usage lower), version 7 takes quite a leap, even outperforming Facebook's HHVM PHP in some benchmarks. While this is of course welcome on a web server, it is *really* noticeable on longer-running programs like typical command-line interface (CLI) scripts.

> *Security*: There have been a few minor security enhancements in version 7, such as the filtering option added to the `unserialize()` function. Overall, the security picture looks broadly the same in terms of the design and implementation of the language, though. One security-related concern to bear in mind is the availability of security patches going forward. Currently patches are available for the 7.0, 5.6, and 5.5 versions. As newer versions are released, though (7.1 is in Alpha stage at the time of writing), the older versions will cease to receive security updates, so if you are sticking with 5.*x* for now, you may want to have a migration plan in mind (assuming you want to continue to use a supported version) for the inevitable upgrade.

> *Features and compatibility*: Version 7 introduced new features and depreciated older ones (you can find full details on the PHP website). None of the CLI-specific features changed, but of course most of the new features are available to use within CLI scripts. The current adoption rate of version 7 appears to be much higher than that of version 5 when it first came out. However, the version 5 series will still be the most commonly installed for some time, so you may want to consider the needs of your audience before using version 7–specific constructs.

If you are careful, both versions can be installed alongside each other. See Appendix A for full details of compiling and installing PHP on various platforms.

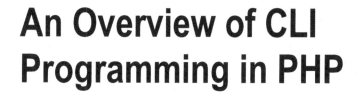

## CHAPTER 2

An Overview of CLI Programming in PHP

Getting Away from the Web

This chapter takes a look at the basic steps involved in breaking free from the Web with PHP. I'll cover the technical steps involved and also the differences in programming practices and focus.

PHP Without a Web Server

Most PHP programmers have used PHP strictly in a web server environment. In such an environment, PHP is a CGI/Fast GGI or server module called and controlled by the HTTP server (usually Apache, IIS, Nginx, or similar). The HTTP server receives a request for a PHP-based web page and calls the PHP process to execute it, which usually returns output to the HTTP server to be sent on to the end user.

There have been a number of attempts to create local applications (scripting systems, desktop apps, and so forth) with PHP using a locally installed web server, with some success. However, the downsides of using this web-type model for local apps are numerous.

- For the value they provide in these scenarios, web servers such as Apache are often over-specified and resource-hungry.

- Unless properly locked down, a web server running locally introduces a point of access to your machine for malicious visitors from the outside world.

- HTTP is a verbose protocol and (arguably) ideally suited for the Web. However, it's often overkill for local interprocess communication and adds another resource and complexity overhead to your application.

- Your application interface typically runs in a web browser and therefore looks anything but local (and comes with additional support/upgrade headaches unless you install a browser specifically for your app).

© Rob Aley 2016
R. Aley, *PHP CLI*, DOI 10.1007/978-1-4842-2238-6_2

PHP, as of version 5.4, includes a built-in web server, which removes some of the problems described earlier. However, it was designed for local testing of PHP scripts designed to be deployed on a fully fledged HTTP server such as Apache in a live environment. It is a route that can be explored for some local apps, particularly where you want to run a private instance of a PHP web app that already exists. However, its stability, reliability, and suitability for production-ready local apps are yet to be proven, and it still comes with the baggage of HTTP and web browsers.

Since version 4.3, PHP has had an ace hidden up its sleeve that solves all of these problems. The PHP CLI Server Application Programming Interface (SAPI), to give it its formal name, is essentially a long way of saying "stand-alone PHP." It cuts out the need for a web server and provides a stand-alone PHP binary for you to interact with. For instance, typing the following at a shell prompt

```
~$ php /home/myfiles/myprogram.php
```

will simply execute your myprogram.php file (which you write mostly like any other PHP script) and return any output to the terminal (unless you tell it otherwise) instead of being sent to the web server (which doesn't exist!).

In general, PHP scripts called directly using the PHP CLI SAPI will behave in the same way as when called through a web server, although there are some differences. For instance, you won't find any $_GET or $_POST arrays, and PHP won't send any HTTP headers by default; these concepts don't mean much beyond the Web. Default settings such as max_execution_time are set to sensible values for local use (in this case to 0 so your scripts won't time out), output buffering is turned off, and error messages are displayed in plain text rather than HTML.

Chapter 3 gives full details of how to install (if necessary) and use the CLI SAPI.

PHP Versions: What's Yours?

PHP has supported the CLI SAPI since version 4.3.0, so many of the examples in this book will run on any PHP version since then. At the time of writing, the current version of PHP is 7.02, and the code in this book has been tested against this version. If you find that a particular function doesn't appear to exist or work as expected, check the online PHP manual for that function. The manual shows which versions support which functions and describes any breaking changes created by newer versions.

If you are using an older version, there are some good reasons to upgrade.

- Performance has increased markedly (and, correspondingly, the resources used have decreased) in recent versions.

- Although security is not always as critical with nonweb applications (see the discussion in "Thinking About Security" later in this chapter for caveats), the security enhancements and security-related bug fixes in recent versions are essential if you're handling data from external sources and if you're using the same version for web work as well.

- Modern language features are available, which can help your coding productivity as well as help others take your code more seriously.

As with the web versions of PHP, you can compile your own version of the CLI SAPI if you find the need. If you want to include extensions not prepackaged by your OS software repositories, remove nonessential code for performance reasons, or use any of the other compile-time options that PHP supports, then learning to "roll your own" version may be worthwhile. You can find a starter guide to compiling and installing PHP and related extensions in Appendix A.

A Few Good Reasons *Not* to Do It in PHP

Tell someone you're going to be writing CLI scripts in PHP and often they'll rail about how PHP is a web language and that you should choose a language "more suited" to the task. This book is focused on doing everything in PHP, and for 90 percent of tasks, PHP will do all that is asked of it. PHP is now a general-purpose language, it's Turing complete, and while it's still used in the main to run "websites," more and more that means back-end services as well. But before you commit to rewrite your world in PHP, there are a few pertinent issues that you may want to consider carefully before jumping in.

High-Performance Requirements

If you need very high performance, particularly on limited hardware, PHP may not be for you. Performance has made leaps and bounds in recent versions of PHP and regularly trounces languages such as Python and frameworks such as Ruby on Rails in benchmarks. However, at its heart PHP is an abstracted scripting language that is never going to get the same performance for some tasks as lower-level languages like C, which are closer to the bare metal. Don't write it off for all high-performance tasks, though; if you're looking at performance with an eye to costs, you may find that the cost savings on developer time through speed of development in PHP outweighs the cost of the extra hardware you throw at it to get the performance. And given that many PHP functions are just wrappers around native C functions and libraries, in some cases (depending on the data structures you are using) performance for parts of your scripts can approach that of C.

Don't (Necessarily) Re-invent the Wheel

You *can* write a web server in PHP, but won't *existing* servers like Apache do what you need? For many or most infrastructure "itches," software exists (written in many different languages) to give you the "scratch" you need. Unless you really need other features, the time spent writing your own is usually going to be greater than the time spent learning and implementing an existing piece of software. Of course, for some people the converse is true. "Because I can" can be a valid reason, and writing software is always a valuable learning experience.

Keeping the Source Closed

PHP is a scripting language, which means if you are writing software to sell or deploy elsewhere, you will be revealing your source code to the recipients. Many (including me) will argue that being open source, even commercially, is a good thing. But if that's not your bag, then you will need to go to greater lengths to protect your code. Source code obfuscators are available online that use various tricks to make your code hard (but not impossible) to read, and a number of PHP compilers are available to produce binary programs (albeit with limitations in terms of syntax and extension coverage). But the main PHP project hasn't expressed any intention to support code hiding or compiling, so the viability of such methods long term is not certain. The business case for closed-source software is also not a done deal in the medium to long term.

Thinking About Security

Every good programmer is at least aware of the security implications of building websites and online apps. You deliberately expose your code to the public, to the world, and to anyone and everyone who will come (good people and bad). One of the early failings of PHP was to prioritize ease of use over security of code (the horror stories from relics like register_globals are only a quick Google search away). With newer, more secure defaults and functions like register_globals being depreciated, PHP is safer than ever online. And although most security problems are caused by the programmer rather than the language, even the newest web coders seem to have an appreciation of security issues from day one these days.

Step into the world of offline software, however, and things are markedly different. Typically we see software for trusted users only, deployed locally on trusted machines and under the full control of the benevolent user. The user isn't going to deliberately attack the software or machine; they're working with their own data. Functionality absolutely can't be compromised. Security is rarely considered at all when developing command-line programs and desktop apps, let alone being features specified at design time, because it's not "necessary."

Except the world doesn't work like that. Take a look at any software vulnerability mailing list like BugTraq and you'll find an abundance of vulnerabilities in "offline" apps such as Adobe Reader, Microsoft Word, and even open-source stalwarts like GIMP. The fact is, security is important even in local apps, for two main reasons. The first is the perennial problem of "typical user" behavior. This is not a problem for an intelligent tech-literate user who never makes mistakes (like you, dear reader), but for any software used by the rest of us disaster is only an accidental-click-on-a-dodgy-e-mail away. The second reason security is important is that for most machines, many nonweb applications aren't really "offline." Even when a desktop app or a system daemon doesn't interact with the Web, local network, or other external services itself, the machine it is connected to will invariably have an Ethernet cable plugged into it or a WiFi/3G/4G connection active. Your software will not run in its own cozy little realm, insulated from the world outside (perfectly sandboxed virtual machines notwithstanding, of course).

Software security is the topic of a whole other book (of which others have written plenty; see the "Further Reading" section), and many of the same principles apply to systems software as to web software, so you will be able to use your existing knowledge of web-based PHP security practices to guide you. The following list of typical vulnerability types and attack vectors in both user-facing and systems software should be considered when planning your script security measures and monitoring:

- *Compromised files from external sources (loaded deliberately or accidentally by users)*: These are usually data files, and particularly at risk is software registered as a default viewer for a particular file type because accidental and malicious file activation is much easier.

- *Malware looking for innocent software to exploit to gain privilege escalation*: Scripted software like PHP code can be easier for malware to rewrite or alter, and the availability of the source code in an uncompiled form can be of help to the malware authors.

- *Legitimate users misbehaving*: John Smith is looking for a way to view the files or surfing history of his boss, Jane Doe, on their shared business system, for instance.

- *Privilege escalation*: Similar to legitimate users misbehaving, this is legitimate software misbehaving, either accidentally or deliberately trying to gain and use access permissions it does not have.

- *PHP vulnerabilities and vulnerabilities in other dependencies and related software*: Your software will be completely free of security issues, of course, but it invariably depends on other libraries, software, and PHP extensions, and of course let's not forget the PHP interpreter. Any of these can contain security bugs and attack vectors.

The previous are common sources of security issues in all types of software, not just in PHP. Minimize your risks by planning for these in the design stage and testing for them before deployment. Then cross your fingers.

Further Reading

- *Securing PHP: Core Concepts* and *Securing PHP: The Usual Suspects* by Chris Cornutt

    - `https://leanpub.com/securingphp-coreconcepts`

    - `https://leanpub.com/securingphp-usualsuspects`

- A free online course in penetration testing; focuses on web-based penetration but relevant also to offline software

    - `https://www.pentesterlab.com/`

- Free online book covering PHP security

    - `http://phpsecurity.readthedocs.org/en/latest/index.html`

- *Building Secure PHP Apps* by Ben Edmunds

    - `https://leanpub.com/buildingsecurephpapps`

CLI-Specific Code Frameworks

There are many coding frameworks for PHP, and many of them can be used with CLI applications, although only one is specifically created for nonweb programming. Code in various frameworks may assume that it will be called in an HTTP-related context, so you may need to do extra work to code around this. When deciding whether to use a framework, or which one to use, you should bear in mind their applicability (in terms of their focus on the Web) and whether your application's performance will suffer from the overhead they may bring. You will usually also need to look at their license because they will usually have components that need to be distributed with your scripts. That's not to say they can't be useful in general-purpose programming; however, there are none that I can at this time recommend specifically for nonweb projects. If you're currently comfortable using a particular framework on your web projects, it may be worth seeing whether there is a "CLI" or "console" module or recommended code path for that particular framework.

Further Reading

- The CLImax CLI-oriented PHP framework
  - *https://github.com/apinstein/climax/*
- The PHP Framework Interop Group, standardizing interoperability between frameworks
  - *http://www.php-fig.org*
- The Symfony Console Component (also used to build the Laravel Artisan Console software)
  - *http://symfony.com/doc/current/components/console/introduction.html*
  - *https://laravel.com/docs/5.1/artisan*
- Zend/Console: Console routes and routing in Zend Framework 2
  - *http://framework.zend.com/manual/current/en/modules/zend.console.routes.html*
- Example of using Zend Framework with a CLI script
  - *http://stackoverflow.com/questions/2325338/running-a-zend-framework-action-from-command-line*
- Framework comparison matrix
  - *http://matrix.include-once.org/framework/*

■ ■ ■

Understanding and Using the CLI SAPI

As mentioned in the previous chapter, PHP CLI scripting involves using the PHP CLI SAPI. It's therefore important to have a good grasp of how to use it, know the options for configuring and running it, and understand how it differs from the web-based SAPIs you are used to using. Luckily, the differences are minimal, and many are intuitive.

What's Different About the CLI SAPI?

The following are the main differences between the CLI SAPI and the standard web implementation:

- No HTTP headers are written to the output by default. This makes sense because they hold no meaning in the command line and so would be just extraneous text printed before your genuine output. If your output will later be funneled out to a web browser, you will need to manually add any necessary headers (for instance, by using the header() PHP function).

- PHP does not change the working directory to that of the PHP script being executed. To do this manually, use getcwd() and chdir() to get and set the current directory. Otherwise, the current working directory will be that from which you invoked the script. For instance, if you are currently in /home/rob and you type php /home/peter/some_script.php, the working directory used in PHP will be /home/rob, not /home/peter.

- Any error or warning messages are output in plain text, rather than HTML-formatted text. If you want HTMLified errors, for instance, if you are producing static HTML files, you can override this by setting the html_errors runtime configuration directive to true in your script using ini_set('html_errors', 1);.

© Rob Aley 2016
R. Aley, *PHP CLI*, DOI 10.1007/978-1-4842-2238-6_3

13

- PHP implicitly "flushes" all output immediately and doesn't buffer by default. Online performance can often be harmed by sending output straight to a browser, so instead output is buffered and sent in optimal-sized chunks when the chunk is full. Offline this is not likely to be an issue, so HTML blocks and output from constructs such as print and echo are sent to the shell straightaway. There is no need to use flush() to clear a buffer when you are waiting for further output. You can still use PHP's output buffering functions to capture and control output if you want; see the "Output Control Functions" section in the PHP manual for more information.

- There is no execution time limit set. Your script will run continuously until it exits of its own volition; PHP will not terminate it even if it hangs. If you want to set a time limit to rein in misbehaving scripts, you can do so from within the script using the set_time_limit() function.

- The variables $argc and $argv, which describe any command-line arguments passed to your script, are automatically set. These are discussed fully later in this chapter.

- PHP defines the constants STDIN, STDOUT, and STDERR, relating to the standard streams of the same name, and automatically opens input/output (I/O) streams for them. These give your application instant access to "standard input" (STDIN), "standard output" (STDOUT), and "standard error" (STDERR) streams.

Further Reading

- "Output Control Functions" section in the PHP manual

  - http://www.php.net/manual/en/ref.outcontrol.php

- "Standard streams" (STDIN, STDOUT, STDERR) on Wikipedia

  - http://en.wikipedia.org/wiki/Standard_streams

CLI SAPI Installation

To use the PHP CLI SAPI, you may need to install it first. Appendix A gives details on installing (and compiling, where necessary) PHP. However, you may find that it is already installed if you have PHP installed (often in a folder called sapi/cli in the PHP program folders), and if not, it is usually available in modern OS software repositories. (For example, in Ubuntu a package called php5-cli exists and can be installed from any package manager or via the command line with sudo apt-get install php5-cli.) If it is installed in the command-line search path, typing php -v on the command line will print the version details, confirming it is indeed installed.

PHP Command-Line Options

The PHP binary will accept a number of command-line options/switches/arguments that affect its operation. You can see a full list by typing php -h. Although some apply only to the CGI SAPI (used when there is not a "module" such as the PHP Apache module), the following are some of the more interesting and common ones used when interacting with the CLI SAPI:

- -f *or* --file: This allows you to specify the file name of the script to be run and is optional. The -f option exists to allow compatibility with software and scripts such as automation software, which can programmatically call command-line programs but require file-name arguments to be formed in this way. It also allows default file-type handlers to be easily set on Windows for PHP scripts. The only real difference in usage between the two versions of the earlier command come when interpreting command-line arguments passed to the script, which we look at in the "Command-Line Arguments for Your Script" section. In most cases, the two following lines are mostly equivalent:

  ```
  ~$ php -f myscript.php
  ~$ php myscript.php
  ```

- -a *or* --interactive: This runs PHP interactively, which allows you to type in PHP code, line by line, rather than executing a saved PHP script. This mode of operation is often called a "REPL" (Read-Eval-Print-Loop). As well as providing an interactive interface for testing and developing code, it can act as an enhanced PHP-enabled shell or command line, and I'll cover this more closely later in this chapter.

- -c *or* --php-ini: This specifies the PHP .ini file that PHP will use for this application. This is particularly useful if you are also running web services using PHP on the same machine; if it is not specified, PHP will look in various default locations for php.ini and may end up using the same one as your web service. By providing one specifically for your CLI applications, you can "open up" various restrictions that make more sense for offline applications. Note that by using the CLI SAPI, PHP will automatically override several php.ini settings regardless of whether you specify a custom .ini file using this option. These overridden settings are those that affect the behavior outlined in the "What's Different About the CLI SAPI?" section, and while the php.ini file is ignored in these cases, you can revert or change these settings directly in your code using the ini_set() function or similar. You can also use the -d or --define option to set options (for example, php -d max_execution_time=2000 myscript.php). If you are deploying software onto machines that you do not control (for example, if you are selling software for users to install on their own machines), it makes sense to use one of these mechanisms to ensure that PHP will be running with the settings you expect, not the settings the user may happen to have. See -n next as well.

- -n *or* --no-php-ini: This tells PHP not to load a php.ini file at all. This can be useful if you do not want to ship one with your application and instead set all of the settings directly within your code using ini_set() or similar. PHP will use its default settings if no .ini file is provided, and it is worth remembering that these default settings may change from version to version of PHP (and indeed have done so in the past). You shouldn't rely on the current defaults being suitable for your application. You can use php --ini to show the default path that PHP will look for .ini files when the -n option isn't used and -c isn't used to specify a file.

- -e *or* --profile-info: This puts PHP into Extended Information Mode (EIM). EIM generates extra information for use by profilers and debuggers. If you're not using a profiler or debugger that requires this mode, you should not enable it because it can degrade performance. You can find more information on profilers and debuggers in Chapter 4.

- -i *or* --info: This calls the phpinfo() function and prints the output. This outputs a *large* range of information about the PHP installation, in plain-text format rather than the usual HTML (it detects you are calling it from the CLI SAPI). This can be useful in tracking down issues with the installation, as well as giving you version information, lists of extensions installed, relevant file paths, and so on. As with any other shell command, the output can be piped to other commands, such as grep. So if you wanted to check whether IPv6 was enabled in your PHP binary for instance, on Linux or OS X you could try the following:

```
~$ php -i | grep -i "ipv6"
```

On Windows you could try the following:

```
> php -i | finstr /I ipv6
```

- -l *or* --syntax-check: This parses the file, checking for syntax errors. This is a basic "lint" type checker; more advanced static code analysis tools are discussed in the next chapter. Be aware that this option checks only for basic syntax errors—the sort that cause the PHP engine to fail. More subtle bugs, problems in your program logic, and errors that are created at run time will not be detected. Your code is not executed, so it can help pick up basic errors before running code that may alter data and cause problems if it fails. Even when you run such code in a testing environment, resetting data and setting up for another test can take time, so a quick check for basic syntax errors first can be a time-saver. Some integrated development environments (IDEs) and text editors run php -l in the background to highlight syntax errors as you type. For instance, the linter-php1 package in GitHub's Atom editor uses this method for live linting of PHP code.

- -m or --modules: This lists all the loaded PHP and Zend modules/ extensions. These are modules that PHP has been compiled with and may include things such as core, mysql, PDO, json, and more. This is useful for checking the PHP installation has the functionality that your application requires. You can also check from within your scripts using the extension_loaded() function or by calling the phpinfo() function. -m provides a subset of the information given with the -i flag described earlier, and -i (or the phpinfo() function) will return more information about the configuration, version, and so on, of the modules.

- -r or --run: This runs a line of PHP code supplied as the argument, rather than executing it from a file. The line of code should be enclosed by single quotes because shells like bash will try to interpolate PHP variables as if they were shell variables if you use double quotes. This performs a similar role to the -a interactive mode, except that PHP's "state" is cleared after each line is executed. This means that the line of code supplied is treated as the whole script to be executed, and execution is terminated once it has been run. Here's an example that will print out "4" followed by a new line character:

```
~$ php -r "echo (2+2).\"\n\";"
```

Note that the line must be well-formed syntactically correct PHP, so don't miss the semicolon at the end! I will return to -r later in this chapter in the section "The Many Ways to Call PHP Scripts."

- -B or --process-begin

-R or --process-code

-F or --process-file

-E or --process-end: These four arguments allow you to specify PHP code to be executed before, during, and after input from STDIN is processed by PHP. -B specifies a line of code to execute before the input is processed, -R specifies a line of code to execute for every line of input, and -F specifies a PHP file to execute for each line. Finally, -E executes a line of code at the end of the input process. In -R and -F, two special variables are available; $argn sets the text of the line being processed, and $argi sets the number of the line being processed. This is mainly useful when using PHP directly in shell scripts. For instance, to print a text file with line numbers, you can do something like this:

```
~$ more my_text_file.txt | php -B "echo \"Lets add line
numbers...\n\";" -R "echo \"$argi: $argn\n\";" -E "echo \"That's
the end folks\n\";"
```

This code will output something like this:

```
Lets add line numbers...
1: Lorem ipsum dolor sit amet, consectetur adipisicing elit, sed do
2: eiusmod tempor incididunt ut labore et dolore magna aliqua. Ut enim ad
3: minim veniam, quis nostrud exercitation ullamco laboris nisi ut aliquip
4: ex ea commodo consequat. Duis aute irure dolor in reprehenderit in
That's the end folks
```

- -s *or* --syntax-highlight: This outputs an HTML version of the PHP script, with colored syntax highlighting. The PHP script is not executed or validated; it's simply made "pretty." The pretty HTML is printed to STDOUT and can be useful when pouring over code looking for errors, issues, and optimizations. This works only with PHP in files, not with code provided by the -r option. Most modern IDEs and code editors provide syntax highlighting by default; however, this can be useful if your only access to a machine is on the command line and the editor you are using doesn't do syntax highlighting. In this case, use -s to create a colored version of your script and either download it or view it through your web browser if the machine has a web server installed.

- -v *or* --version: This outputs the PHP version information. This can also be found in the output of the -i option described earlier. Be careful when assuming a particular format; some package repositories (Ubuntu, for instance) include their name and their own build numbers in the version string, so don't just filter it for any numerics.

- -w *or* --strip: This outputs the contents of the source code with any unnecessary white space and any comments removed. This can be used only with code files (not with lines of code supplied by -r) and does not work with the syntax highlighting option shown earlier. This is used to "minify" a file, in other words, reduce the file size. Contrary to popular opinion, this will not speed up most scripts; the overhead of parsing comments and white space is extremely negligible. You should also be wary of support and debugging issues, even if a copy of the "full" code is kept, as line numbers in error reports will no longer match between the original and stripped versions. It also does not minify identifies such as variable names and so cannot be used to obfuscate your code. There are few reason to use this option these days. To make a file smaller for distribution, using proper compression (for example, adding it to a zip file) is usually a better method.

- -z *or* --zend-extension: This specifies the file name/path for a Zend extension to be loaded before your script is run. This allows dynamic loading of extensions, which can alternatively be specified in the php.ini file if they are always to be loaded.

- --rf *or* --rfunction

  --rc *or* --rclass

  --re *or* --rextension

  --rz *or* --rzendextension

  --ri *or* --rextinfo: These options allow you to explore PHP structures using reflection. Reflection is the process by which PHP can perform runtime *introspection*, which is the means to allow you to look into elements and structures of your code at run time. The first three options print reflection information about a named function, class, or extension. The last two print basic information about a Zend extension or a standard extension, as returned by the phpinfo() function. This reflection information, which is very detailed, is available only if PHP is compiled with reflection support. These options can be used as a quick but precise reference guide to the entities listed earlier and are particularly useful in interrogating unknown code written by others.

Further Reading

- Reflection information in the PHP manual

  - *http://www.php.net/manual/en/book.reflection.php*

- "Introspection and Reflection in PHP" by Octavia Anghel

  - *http://www.sitepoint.com/introspection-and-reflection-in-php/*

Command-Line Arguments for Your Script

As you've seen, passing arguments to PHP is straightforward and done in the normal way. However, passing arguments for use by your PHP script is a little more complicated, as PHP needs to know where its own arguments stop and where your script's start. The best way to examine how PHP deals with this is through some examples. Consider the following PHP script:

```
<?

echo "Number of arguments given :".$argc."\n";

echo "List of arguments given :\n";

print_r($argv);
```

There are two special variables in the previous script.

- $argc: This records the number of command-line arguments passed to the script.

- $argv: This is an array of the actual arguments passed.

Let's save the script as arguments.php. Now let's call it as follows:

```
~$ php -e arguments.php -i -b=big -l red white "and blue"
```

You will get the following output:

```
Number of arguments given :7
List of arguments given :
Array
(
    [0] => arguments.php
    [1] => -i
    [2] => -b=big
    [3] => -l
    [4] => red
    [5] => white
    [6] => and blue
)
```

As you can see, all the arguments given from the file name onward in the command are passed to the script. The first, -e, which is used by PHP itself, is not passed through. So, as a general rule, everything after the file name is treated as an argument to the script, anything before the file name is treated as an argument for PHP itself, and the file name is shared between the two.

There is, of course, an exception. As you learned earlier, in addition to specifying the file name of your script on its own, you can also pass it as part of the -f flag. So if you execute the following command

```
~$ php -e -f arguments.php -i -b=big -l red white "and blue"
```

you get the following unexpected output:

```
phpinfo()
PHP Version => 5.4.6-1ubuntu1.3

System => Linux dev-system 3.5.0-37-generic #58-Ubuntu SMP Mon Jul 8
22:10:28 UTC 2013 i686
Build Date => Jul 15 2013 18:23:34
Server API => Command Line Interface
Virtual Directory Support => disabled
Configuration File (php.ini) Path => /etc/php5/cli
<rest of output removed for brevity>
```

You may recognize this as the output of calling php -i. Rather than treating arguments after the file name as belonging to the script, PHP has treated the -i argument (and those afterward) as one of its own. As -i is a valid PHP argument, it decides that it was what you wanted and invokes its "information" mode. If you need to pass the file name as part of the -f flag rather than as an argument on its own, you will need to separate your scripts arguments using two dashes (--). So, for the previous command to work as expected, you need to alter it to read as follows:

```
~$ php -e -f arguments.php -- -i -b=big -l red white "and blue"
```

Everything after the --, plus the script file name, is passed as arguments to the script, and you get the expected output.

This can make your scripts a little messy, particularly if you are passing lots of arguments, so you may want to look at the sections below on self executing scripts, which show you how to embed PHPs arguments within the script, allowing the script to claim any and all arguments passed as its own.

The Many Ways to Call PHP Scripts

As you can probably tell from the command-line options in the previous section, there are several ways to execute PHP code when using the CLI SAPI. Although I've covered a couple of these already, I will discuss them here again for completeness.

From a File

You can tell PHP to execute a particular PHP source code file. Here's an example:

```
~$ php myscript.php
~$ php -f myscript.php
```

Note that -f is optional; the previous two lines are functionally equivalent. The PHP command-line options detailed earlier, where appropriate, work in this method. This example

```
~$ php -e myscript.php
```

will execute the file myscript.php in Extended Information Mode.

As with the web version of PHP, source files can be interpolated (mixed) with HTML (or, more usefully on the command line, plain text). So, you will still need your opening <? or <?php tags; otherwise, your source code will just be printed straight out without being executed.

From a String

You can execute a single line of code with the -r flag, as shown here:

```
~$ php -r "echo(\"Hello World!\n\");"
```

Many of the other command-line options are not available with the -r method, such as syntax highlighting. Watch out for shell variable substitution (use single quotes rather than double quotes around your code) and other mangling of your code by the shell. Unless it really is a quick one-off, it is likely safer and easier to pop the relevant line into a file and execute that instead. One common use of the -r option is for executing PHP generated by other (possibly non-PHP) shell commands where the whole shell script needs to execute in memory without touching the disk (for instance, where permissions prohibit disk write access).

From STDIN

If you do not specify a file or use the -r option, PHP will treat the contents of STDIN as the PHP code to be executed, as shown here (note echo only works like this on Linux or OS X):

```
~$ echo '<? echo "hello\n";?>' | php
```

You can also use this method with -B, -R, -F, and -E to make PHP a first-class citizen in shell scripting, giving you the ability to pipe data in and out of PHP. For instance, to reverse every line of a file (or any data source that you pipe into it), on Linux or OS X use the following:

```
~$ cat file.txt | php -R 'echo strrev($argn)."\n";' | grep olleh
```

On Windows use the following:

```
> more file.txt | php -R "echo strrev($argn).\"\n\";" | findstr olleh
```

In this line of code, you pipe the contents of a text file into PHP. The -R option tells PHP to execute the following PHP code on each line of input, where the line is stored in the special variable $argn. In this case, you reverse $argn using the string-reversing function strrev() and then echo the reversed string out again. Any echo'd output goes to STDOUT, which either is printed to the shell or, as in this case, can be piped to another shell command. In this case, you then use grep to display only the lines containing the string olleh, which is *hello* backward. You can find more details on -R and its siblings in the previous section.

If you want to use options like -R but have too much PHP code to fit comfortably on the command line, you can put the code in a normal PHP source code file and include it with include(). Here's an example:

```
~$ cat something.txt > php -R 'include("complicated.php");'
```

If it is a nontrivial PHP script, it may be more efficient to package it up into functions and include it once with -B (-B means it's executed before the main code) and then execute the function each time with -R. The following example loads the content of my_functions.php once at the start, and then the function complicated() from that file is called on each line (each $argn) from the data file (data.txt).

```
~$ php -B 'include("my_functions.php");' -R 'complicated($argn);' -f
'data.txt'
```

Although these commands look relatively simple, there is of course no arbitrary limit to the PHP code you can put behind them. You can use classes and objects, multiple files, and most of the code and techniques explored in this book, exposing only functions or methods at the shell level as an interface for the user. You can also open the standard streams as PHP streams within PHP and access their file pointers to read data in from, negating the need to use -R, as discussed in the next chapter.

As a Self-executing Script: Unix/Linux

On Unix/Linux systems you can turn a PHP script file into a directly executable shell command. Simply make the first line of the script file a #! line (usually pronounced "shebang line" or "hashbang line") with a path to the PHP binary, as in this example:

```
#!/usr/bin/php
<?

echo('Hello World!');
```

Then set the executable bit using chmod or similar. Here's an example:

```
~$ chmod a+x myscript.php
```

Simply typing ./myscript.php at the command line will execute it. You can also rename the file to remove the .php extension (assuming you had one in the first place), so you would just type the following at the shell prompt to run it:

```
~$ ./myscript
```

You can further simplify it to remove the initial ./ by moving it to a directory somewhere in your shell's search path. Note that when running a script in this manner, any command-line options are passed directly to the script and not to PHP. In fact, you cannot pass extra command-line parameters to PHP at runtime using this method; you must include them in the shebang line when constructing your script. For instance, in the previous example, if you wanted to use Extended Information Mode, you would alter the first line of the script to read as follows:

```
#!/usr/bin/php -e
```

If you were to instead call the script as follows

```
~$ myscript -e
```

then the -e flag would be passed as an argument to the script, not to PHP directly, and so PHP would not enter EIM. This is useful for scripts that have lots of user-supplied arguments but also makes options like -B and -R discussed in the previous method cumbersome to use for processing STDIN data because you have to include all the PHP on the shebang line where it is harder to change. However, you can simply use include() to include the necessary files and use standard file streams to process the STDIN stream (created and opened by the CLI SAPI automatically for you) line by line instead.

If your script may be used on other systems, please bear in mind that the PHP binary will quite often be located in a different directory than the one on your system. In this scenario, you will need to change the shebang line for each system if you hard-code the location in it. Fortunately, if installed correctly, PHP sets an environment variable with its location, available via the /usr/bin/env shell command. So if you change the shebang line as follows, your script should be executable wherever PHP is located:

```
#!/usr/bin/env php
```

On Windows, the shebang line can be left in because PHP will recognize it and ignore it. However, it will not execute the file as it does on *nix.

Further Reading

- Standard I/O streams information in the PHP manual

    - *http://php.net/manual/en/features.commandline.io-streams.php*

As a Self-executing Script: Windows

In a similar manner, scripts can be executed by calling them directly under Windows. However, the process for setting up Windows to do this is slightly more involved.

First, you need to add your PHP directory (the directory containing php.exe, php-win.exe, or php-cli.exe) to the Windows search path (specified in the environment variable PATH) so that you can call PHP without having to specify the full directory path. To do this, follow these steps:

1. From the Start menu, go to the Control Panel and select the System icon from the System and Security group.

2. On the Advanced tab, click the Environment Variables button.

3. In the System Variables pane, find the Path entry (you may need to scroll to find it).

4. Double-click the Path entry to edit it and add your PHP directory at the end, including a semicolon (;) before it (for example, ;C:\php). Make sure that you do not overwrite or remove any of the text already in the path box.

You also need to amend the PATHEXT environment variable in the same way, so find the PATHEXT entry in the same window and add .PHP, again using a semicolon to separate it from the rest of the entries while taking care not to alter them.

Next you need to associate the .php file extension with a file type and then tell Windows which program to run for files of that type. To do this, run the following two commands in the Windows command prompt, which you should run as administrator. Make sure to change the path/file name in the second command to match your installation.

```
assoc .php=phpfile
ftype phpfile="C:\PHP5\php.exe" -f "%1" -- %~2
```

These changes will allow you to run myscript rather than C:\php\php.exe myscript.php. Note that under Windows 10 you will not be able to run scripts in this way in an elevated (administrator) command prompt because the PHP executable is not run as administrator by default. To fix this, right-click the php.exe executable, select Properties and Compatibility, and select "Run this program as an administrator" in Settings. Apply the change to all users. Scripts should now execute as expected in all command prompts.

Windows php-win.exe

PHP for Windows also ships with php-win.exe, which is similar to the CLI build of PHP, except that it does not open a command-line window. This is useful for running system software in the background or running scripts that create their own graphical interface.

Quitting Your Script

You've looked at starting your scripts, but what happens when it comes time to finish running them?

Like web-based PHP scripts, CLI scripts will terminate happily when you hit the end of the script file and will tidy up all the resources used in the same way. Likewise, if you want to end early, you can call the exit (or equivalent die) language construct.

However, in the world of CLI scripts, this isn't considered very polite. Because CLI command are designed to work together, often in chains of commands, most shell programs and scripts will provide an "exit code" when they terminate to let the other programs around them know *why* they finished. Were they done? Did they encounter an error? Were they called incorrectly? Inquiring minds want to know.

It is particularly important to supply an exit code when your script may be the last item in a shell script, as the exit code of the shell script as a whole is taken to be the last exit code returned within it. You can make your PHP script provide an exit code simply by including it as a parameter to exit or die. An exit code is an integer, and there are a number of common exit codes.

- 0: Success. You've exited normally.

- 1: General error. This is usually used for application/language-specific errors and syntax errors.

- 2: Incorrect usage.

- 126: Command is not executable. This is usually permissions related.

- 127: Command not found.

- 128+N (up to 165): Command terminated by POSIX signal number N. For example, in the case of kill -9 myscript.php, it should return code 137 (128+9).

- 130: Command terminated by Ctrl-C (Ctrl-C is POSIX code 2, so, as earlier, 128 + 2 = 130).

Further Reading

- "POSIX signals" on Wikipedia

    - http://en.wikipedia.org/wiki/Unix_signal#POSIX_signals

Any other positive integer is generally construed as exiting because of an unspecified error. So, for instance, if you decide the command-line arguments provided by your user are not in the correct format, you should terminate your script using exit(2). If instead all goes well and your script continues to the end of its script file, you can actually let it exit by itself (or by calling exit without a parameter) because it returns status code 0 by default.

As with web scripts, you can register functions to be executed when your PHP script exits using the `register_shutdown_function()` function. One use for this may be to check that all is well and evaluate which exit code should be returned. The exit code used as the parameter to `exit` or `die` within a registered shutdown function overrides the code used in the initial exit call that initiated shutdown. This means you can happily exit with `exit(0)` everywhere and then exit with `exit(76)` from your shutdown function if you detect that the foo conflaganation isn't aligned with the bar initispations in your metaspacialatific object. Or similar.

PHP REPLs

When you want to test a few lines of PHP, your default instinct may be to create a new PHP file, save it, and then execute it with PHP. There is a better, faster, and more interactive way, however. The PHP "interactive shell," also known as the PHP REPL, is a quick and easy way to type in code and have it execute immediately. Unlike executing single lines of code using `php -r`, the REPL (started by calling `php -a`) keeps the script's state (for example, contents of variables and objects) in between each line that you type until you exit. You can use all of PHP's functions, although no libraries are loaded by default, and you can use `include()` or `require()` to include existing files of PHP code. This latter capability is useful for debugging the final output of a problematic script; simply use `include()` to include your script, which will execute the script, and as long the script doesn't terminate prematurely, then you can use `echo()` or `print_r()` (or otherwise) to explore the state of the variables and other resources at the end of the run. Other brands of REPL are available and are listed later in this section. By its nature, it can also be used as a CLI/shell in its own right, calling other PHP and non-PHP programs as you would in, for instance, a bash shell.

The following example is a capture of an actual interactive REPL session using the standard PHP REPL:

```
~$ php -a
Interactive shell

php > # As we can type any valid PHP, I have added comments
php > # directly to the REPL, rather than afterwards in editing!
php >
php > # Lets start with some simple assignments :
php >
php > $a = 5;
php > $b = 6;
php >
php > # The REPL will throw Notices, Warnings and Errors as appropriate,
php > # in real-time :
php >
php > $c = nothingdefined;
PHP Notice:  Use of undefined constant nothingdefined - assumed
'nothingdefined' in php shell code on line 1
php >
```

27

```
php > # Just as with normal PHP source files, we can split commands across
php > # lines. The interpreter only kicks in when it hits the terminating
php > # semicolon :
php >
php > $d
php > =
php > 7
php > ;
php >
php > # The following shows that the state in the variables above has been
php > # kept :
php >
php > echo $a + $b + $c + $d ."\n";
18
php >
php > # Next, a more interesting example. Use the REPL instead of the
php > # shell to get the first line from a file :
php >
php > echo file ('/proc/version')[0];
Linux version 3.5.0-21-generic (buildd@roseapple) (gcc version 4.7.2
(Ubuntu/Linaro 4.7.2-2ubuntu1) ) #32-Ubuntu SMP Tue Dec 11 18:52:46 UTC
2012
php >
php > # Of course all of the usual protocol wrappers are available, so we
php > # can see what is happening in the world...
php >
php > $page = file ('http://news.bbc.co.uk');
php >
php > echo $page[0];
<!DOCTYPE html PUBLIC "-//W3C//DTD XHTML+RDFa 1.0//EN" "http://www.w3.org/
MarkUp/DTD/xhtml-rdfa-1.dtd">
php >
php > # and maybe get a hash of that...
php >
php > echo md5 ( implode ( $page, "\n" ) ) . "\n";
0319bf4e62db39fb2c89210e48783d70
php >
php > # when we are done ...
php >
php > exit;
php >
php > # doesn't work, as its just evaluated as PHP (and the REPL ignores
php > # exit/die calls. To exit the REPL, enter the word 'exit' on its own
php > # on a new line
php >
php > exit
~$
```

Sometimes you'll want to execute your commands within the "environment" of other scripts. For instance, you may have a script that declares constants, sets up database connections, and does other routine tasks that you normally include with include() at the start of your main PHP scripts. As noted earlier, you can include these files in the REPL too using include(), but you may forget to do so and then wonder why things didn't work as they should. One facility PHP offers you, which applies not only to the REPL but to all forms of PHP execution, is the auto_prepend_file configuration directive. This tells PHP to execute a given file each time PHP is run before it starts to do anything else (such as executing the script you have asked it to execute). This can be set either in php.ini or via the -d flag on the command line. The following is an example of presetting some constants/variables. First, you create a script called initialise.php with the following content:

```php
<?php

const FOUR = 4; # Declare a constant value

$five = 5; # Instantiate a variable with another value
```

Then, at the command line, start and run a REPL session as follows, using -d to execute the initialise.php script first:

```
~$ php -d auto_prepend_file=initialise.php -a
Interactive shell

php > echo (FOUR + $five)."\n";
9
php > exit
~$
```

As you can see, the constant and variable you had set up in the initialise.php file were available for use from the REPL without having to manually declare them. The -d flag is used here, but the option could be set in php.ini as well if you want to always use the same file. If you regularly use a few different initialization files like this, you can create shell aliases to commands using the -d flag. For instance, you could add lines similar to the following to your ~/.bash_profile:

```
alias php-cl="php -d auto_prepend_file=clientSetup.php -a"
alias php-in="php -d auto_prepend_file=ourSiteSetup.php -a"
```

As well as the built-in PHP REPL explored earlier, there are a number of third-party REPLs available, some of which include features such as a history of commands typed, tab-completion of commands, protection from fatal errors, and even abbreviated function documentation.

Toolbox	phpsh

Developed at Facebook, phpsh is an interactive shell for PHP that features readline history, tab completion, and quick access to documentation.

Main website and documentation	`http://phpsh.org`
Installation information	`https://github.com/facebook/phpsh/blob/master/README.md`

Toolbox	Boris

A small but robust REPL for PHP

Main documentation and installation information	`https://github.com/d11wtq/boris`
Extension for Symfony and Drupal	`http://vvv.tobiassjosten.net/php/php-repl-for-symfony-and-drupal/`

Toolbox	phpa

A simple replacement for `php -a`, written in PHP

Main website, installation information and documentation	`http://david.acz.org/phpa/`

Toolbox	PHP Interactive

A web-based REPL that allows better support of displaying HTML output. The project is an Alpha release.

Main website	`http://www.hping.org/phpinteractive/`

Toolbox	Sublime-worksheet

An inline REPL for the Sublime Text editor

Main website	`https://github.com/jcartledge/sublime-worksheet`

Toolbox	iPHP

An extensible PHP shell

Main website	`https://github.com/apinstein/iphp`

CHAPTER 4

User-Facing Software

After slugging through the preliminary information necessary to understand developing PHP in a nonweb context, you're now getting to the nitty-gritty of how to start communicating with your users without the rendering engine of a web browser.

Command-Line Interface Basics

Although graphical interfaces seem to garner the most attention these days, there are still plenty of uses for text-based interfaces, particularly in environments with technically adept users. When creating a text-based program to run on the command line, there are three primary considerations over and above the PHP you are already accustomed to.

- Getting keyboard input
- Outputting text (and graphics) to the screen
- Program flow control

Rather than learn about each one in isolation, you will instead look at a simple program that contains elements of each. Read through the following code and comments. The program is a screen-saver type of routine that fills the shell with color via a wiggling snake-like cursor.

```php
<?php

# First we will define some named constants.
# These are shell escape codes, used for formatting
# Defining them as named constants helps to make our code more readable.

define("ESC", "\033");
define("CLEAR", ESC."[2J");
define("HOME", ESC."[0;0f");

# We will output some instructions to the user. Note that we use
# fwrite rather than echo. The aim is to write our output back to the
# shell where the user will see it. fwrite(STDOUT... writes to the
```

© Rob Aley 2016
R. Aley, *PHP CLI*, DOI 10.1007/978-1-4842-2238-6_4

```
# php://stdout stream. Echo (and print) write to the php://output
# stream. Usually these are both the same thing, but they don't have to
# be. Additionally php://output is subject to the Output control &
# buffering functions (http://www.php.net/manual/en/book.outcontrol.php)
# which may or may not be desirable.

fwrite(STDOUT, "Press Enter To Begin, And Enter Again To End");

# Now we wait for the user to press enter. By default, STDIN is
# a blocking stream, which means that when we try to read from it,
# our script will stop and wait some input. Keyboard input to the shell
# is passed to our script (via fread) when the user presses Enter.

fread(STDIN,1);

# We want the program to run until the user presses enter again. This
# means that we want to periodically check for input with fread, but not
# to pause/block the program if there isn't any input. So we set STDIN to
# be non-blocking.

stream_set_blocking(STDIN, 0);

# In preparation for our output, we want to clear the terminal and draw a
# pretty frame around it. To do this we need to know how big the terminal
# window currently is. There is no in-built way to do this, so we call an
# external shell command called tput, which gives information about the
# current terminal.

$rows = intval(`tput lines`);
$cols = intval(`tput cols`);

# We now write two special escape codes to the terminal, the first
# of which (\033[2J) clears the screen, the second of which (\033[0;0f)
# puts the cursor at the top left of the screen. We've already defined
# these as the constants CLEAR and HOME at the start of the script

fwrite(STDOUT, CLEAR.HOME);

# Now we want to draw a frame around our window. The simplest way to draw
# "graphics" (or "semigraphics") in the terminal is to use box drawing
# characters that are included with most fixed-width fonts used in
# terminals.

# Draw the vertical frames by moving the cursor step-by-step down each
# side. The cursor is moved with the escape code generated by
# ESC."[$rowcount;1f"
```

```
for ($rowcount = 2; $rowcount < $rows; $rowcount++) {
  fwrite(STDOUT, ESC."[$rowcount;1f"."║"); # e.g. \033[7;1f║ for line 7
  fwrite(STDOUT, ESC."[$rowcount;${cols}f"."║");
}

# Now do the same for the horizontal frames.

for ($colcount = 2; $colcount < $cols; $colcount++) {
  fwrite(STDOUT, ESC."[1;${colcount}f"."=");
  fwrite(STDOUT, ESC."[$rows;${colcount}f"."=");
}

# And finally fill in the corners.

fwrite(STDOUT, ESC."[1;1f"."╔");
fwrite(STDOUT, ESC."[1;${cols}f"."╗");
fwrite(STDOUT, ESC."[$rows;1f"."╚");
fwrite(STDOUT, ESC."[$rows;${cols}f"."╝");

# You can see the range of box drawing characters available at
# http://en.wikipedia.org/wiki/Box-drawing_character
# They are just "text" like any other character, so you can easily copy
# and paste them into most editors.

# $p is an array [x,y] that holds the position of our cursor. We will
# initialise it to be the centre of the screen.

$p = ["x"=>intval($cols/2), "y"=>intval($rows/2)];

# Now for our first element of flow control. We need to keep the program
# running until the user provides input. The simplest way to do this is to
# use a never-ending loop using while(1). "1" always evaluates to true, so
# the while loop will never end. When we (or the user) are ready to end
# the program, we can use the "break" construct to step out of the loop
# and continue the remaining script after the end of the loop.

while (1) {

# Each time we go through the loop, we want to check if the user has
# pressed enter while we were in the last loop. Remember that STDIN is
# no longer blocking, so if there is no input the program continues
# immediately. If there is input we use break to leave the while loop.

  if (fread(STDIN,1)) { break; };

# We will step the position of the cursor, stored in $p, by a random
# amount in both the x and y axis. This makes our snake crawl!
```

```
$p['x'] = $p['x'] + rand(-1,1);
$p['y'] = $p['y'] + rand(-1,1);
```

```
# We check that our snake won't step onto or over the frame, to keep
# it in its box!
```

```
if ($p['x'] > ($cols-1)) { $p['x'] = ($cols-1);};
if ($p['y'] > ($rows-1)) { $p['y'] = ($rows-1);};
if ($p['x'] < 2) { $p['x'] = 2;};
if ($p['y'] < 2) { $p['y'] = 2;};
```

```
# We want a pretty trail, so we need to pick random colours for the
# foreground and background colour of our snake, that change at
# each step. Colours in the terminal are set with yet more escape
# codes, from a limited palette, specified by integers.
```

```
$fg_color = rand(30,37);
$bg_color = rand(40,47);
```

```
# Once chosen, we set the colours by outputting the escape codes. This
# doesn't immediately print anything, it just sets the colour of
# whatever else follows.
```

```
fwrite(STDOUT, ESC."[${fg_color}m"); # \033[$32m sets green foreground
fwrite(STDOUT, ESC."[${bg_color}m"); # \033[$42m sets green background
```

```
# Finally we output a segment of snake (another box drawing character)
# at the new location. It will appear with the colours we just set, at
# the location stored in $p
```

```
fwrite(STDOUT, ESC."[${p['y']};${p['x']}f"."╬");
```

```
# Before we let the while loop start again, we need to do one more
# very important thing. We need to give your processor a rest.
# If we just continued our loop straight away, you would find your
# processor being hammered, just for our relatively simple program.
# Our snake would also consume the screen at super-speed!
# usleep pauses execution of the program, so others can use the
# processor or the processor can "rest". Every little bit helps the
# responsiveness of your machine, so even if you need your program
# to loop as fast as possible, consider even a small usleep if you can
```

```
usleep(1000);
};
```

```
# If this line of code has been reached, it means that we have 'break'd
# from the while loop.
```

```
# To be a good citizen of the terminal, we need to clean up the screen
# before we exit. Otherwise, the cursor will remain on which-ever line
# our snake left it, and the background/foreground colours will be
# the last ones chosen for our snake segment.

# The following escape code tells the terminal to use its default colours.

fwrite(STDOUT, ESC."[0m");

# We then clear the screen and put the cursor at the top-left, as we
# did earlier.

fwrite(STDOUT, CLEAR.HOME);
```

This program should demonstrate the three basics listed earlier.

- *Getting keyboard input*: You can read from STDIN in the same way you would any stream.

- *Outputting text (and graphics) to the screen*: You can output to STDOUT (or use echo/print), control the appearance and cursor with escape characters, and use block drawing characters to make "semigraphics."

- *Program flow control*: A while(1) loop is useful for keeping a program running, with break to continue flow outside the loop. It's important to use usleep or sleep to stop your process from hogging a processor.

Advanced Command-Line Input

The previous section showed how to use fread() to read keyboard input. This is suitable for simple programs, but if you are looking to create a more complex interface to allow users to issue commands, then you may want to look at the readline extension, which you can use to implement a shell-like editable command-line program. Unfortunately, for Windows users, the readline library works only under Linux and Unix, and there is nothing comparable for the Windows platform.

The following example script shows how to implement a simple bespoke command-line type interface with the readline library:

```
<?php

# Create arrays to hold our command history and list of valid commands.

$history = array();
$validCommands = array();

# Define some valid commands.
```

```php
$validCommands[] = 'kill';
$validCommands[] = 'destroy';
$validCommands[] = 'obliterate';
$validCommands[] = 'history';
$validCommands[] = 'byebye';

# We want to enable tab-completion of commands, which allows the user to
# start typing a command and then press tab to have it completed, as
# happens in Bash shells and the like. We need to provide a function (via
# readline_completion_function) that will provide an array of possible
# functions names. This can be based on the $partial characters the user
# has typed or the point in the program we are at, or any other
# factors we want. In our case, we'll simply provide an array of ALL of
# the valid commands we have.

function tab_complete ($partial) {
  global $validCommands;
  return $validCommands;
};

readline_completion_function('tab_complete');

# We now enter our main program loop. Note that we don't include a usleep,
# as readline pauses our program execution while it waits for input from
# the user.

while (1) {

# We call readline with a string that forms the command prompt. In our
# case we'll put the date & time in there to show that we can change
# it each time it's called. Whatever the user enters is returned. This
# one simple line implements most of the readline magic. At this stage
# the user can take advantage of tab-completion, history (use up/down
# cursor keys) and so on.

  $line = readline(date('H:i:s')." Enter command > ");

# We need to manually add commands to the history. This is used for
# the command history that the user accesses with the up/down cursor
# keys. We could choose to ignore commands (mis-typed ones or
# intermediate input, for example) if we want.

  readline_add_history($line);

# If we want to programmatically retrieve the history, we can use a
# function called readline_list_history(). However, this is only
# available if PHP has been compiled using libreadline. In most cases,
# modern distributions compile it using the compatible libedit library
```

```
# for licensing and other reasons. So we will keep a parallel copy of
# the history in an array for programatic access.

$history[] = $line;

# Now we decide what to do with the users input. In real life, we may
# want to trim(), strtolower() and otherwise filter the input first.

  switch ($line) {

    case "kill":
        echo "You don't want to do that.\n";
        break;

    case "destroy":
        echo "That really isn't a good idea.\n";
        break;

    case "obliterate":
        echo "Well, if we really must.\n";
        break;

    case "history":

# We will use the parallel copy of the command history that we
# created earlier to display the command history.

        $counter = 0;

        foreach($history as $command) {
          $counter++;
          echo("$counter: $command\n");
        };

        break;

    case "byebye":

# If it's time to leave, we want to break from both the switch
# statement and the while loop, so we break with a level of 2.

        break 2;

    default :

# Always remember to give feedback in the case of user error.

    echo("Sorry, command ".$line." was not recognised.\n");
```

```
    }

};

# If we reached here, the user typed byebye.

echo("Bye bye, come again soon!\n");
```

You may have noticed that I chose to use byebye as the command to quit the program. This was not just a whimsical choice on my part but to illustrate the need to think about discoverability. If you were presented with this program, without seeing the previous source code, and asked to close it, it's likely you would try quit, exit, end, and so on, before resorting to a good old Ctrl-C. In a GUI interface, you would have no such problems when faced with a button that said "Bye Bye!" With text-based input, it is best to stick to common and memorable formats for commands, provide visual guidance and clues where possible, and aid in discoverability with good documentation, a help command, and user training.

Further Reading

- Readline extension in the PHP manual

  - http://www.php.net/manual/en/intro.readline.php

Using STDIN, STOUT, and STDERR

The PHP CLI SAPI automatically opens the standard streams for you when your script starts, so there is no need to issue commands like fopen('php://stdin', 'r'). You can treat these streams just like any other PHP stream and start using them straightaway. You saw some examples earlier, but here are a few more to illustrate the options available:

```php
<?php

# Get one line of input from STDIN

echo ('Please Type Something In : >');

$line1 = fgets(STDIN);

echo ('**** Line 1 : '.$line1." ****\n\n");

# Get one line of input, without the newline character

echo ('Please Type Something Else In : >');

$line2 = trim(fgets(STDIN));
```

```php
echo ('**** Line 2 : '.$line2." ****\n\n");

# Write an array out to STDOUT in CSV format.
# First, create an array of arrays...

$records[] = array('User', 'Full Name', 'Gender');
$records[] = array('Rob', 'Rob Aley', 'M');
$records[] = array('Ada', 'Augusta Ada King, Countess of Lovelace', 'F');
$records[] = array('Grete', 'Grete Hermann', 'F');

echo ("The following is your Data in CSV format :\n\n");

# ...then convert each array to CSV on the fly as we write it out

foreach ($records as $record) {

  fputcsv(STDOUT, $record);

};

echo ("\n\nEnd of your CSV data\n");

# Pause until the user enters something starting with a number

echo ('Please type one or more numbers : >');

while (! fscanf(STDIN, "%d\n", $your_number) ) {

  echo ("No numbers found :>");

};

echo ("Your number was $your_number\n\n");

# Send the text of a web page to STDOUT

echo ("Press enter for some interwebs :\n\n");

fread(STDIN, 1); # fread blocks until enter pressed

fwrite(STDOUT, strip_tags( file_get_contents('http://www.cam.ac.uk') ) );

# Send an error message to STDERR. You can just fwrite(STDERR,...
# if you want, or you can use the error_log function, which uses the
# defined error handling routine. By default for the CLI SAPI this is
# printing to STDERR.

error_log('System ran out of beer. ABORT. ABORT.', 4);
```

The error logged on the last line will usually appear in your shell along with the other output because that is where most shells put STDERR by default. If you want to check that it did come via STDERR rather than STDOUT, the following bash command will highlight any STDERR output (denoted by the 2>) in red. It uses escape codes to color the error (31 sets the color to red, 07 reverses it, and then 0 clears it).

```
~$ php script.php 2> >(while read errors; do echo -e "\e[07;31m$errors\e
[0m" >&2;  done)
```

In short, you can use the standard streams in any number of ways, often treating them as standard file pointers or streams.

CLI Helper Libraries

There are some prewritten libraries/components available that can take some of the effort out of creating interactive console software. I've listed three common ones in this section. As with most libraries of this type, they are quite "opinionated" in how your program should be structured, so do look thoroughly through the documentation of each before choosing which best suits your project. The Symfony console (part of the Symfony Framework project) is well-tested and stable; as with most Symfony components, it is well-documented and supported. If you are familiar with the Symfony Framework, then the code style should be familiar, but it is equally at home with other frameworks (it is used for the Laravel Framework Artisan Console tool). The Webmozart Console toolkit is a refactored version of the Symfony Console component so has similar features but a different coding style. It is also currently still in Beta. Finally, the Hoa Console is perhaps the most distinct of the three, with a coding style that focuses on real-world tasks and is arguably easier to get to grips with as a developer.

Toolbox	Symfony Console
The Console component of the Symfony PHP Framework project	
Main website	https://github.com/symfony/Console

Toolbox	Webmozart Console
A (Beta) Console component refactored from the Symfony Console	
Main website	https://github.com/webmozart/console

Toolbox	The Hoa\Console Library
A Console library aimed at industrial and research use	
Main website	https://github.com/hoaproject/Console

CHAPTER 5

■ ■ ■

PHP CLI Scripts and Your System

PHP CLI scripts typically interact with your system in a number of areas. While most system interactions are identical to those you're used to with web scripts, there are a few areas you may not have used much, so I'll cover a few gotchas that might trip you up.

Starting External Processes from PHP, or "Shelling Out"

A common feature of CLI scripts is calling and interacting with other scripts and processes. Using other scripts and programs as "building blocks" within your script is a common pattern of CLI programming. As you saw earlier, you can often combine your PHP script with others in general-purpose shell scripts, but often it is useful for the PHP script itself to start other software when it needs to do so. This is often referred to as *shelling out*.

A number functions are available in PHP to achieve this, each doing it in a slightly different way and with different benefits.

- exec(): Executes a program and sends the text output to the user.

- passthru(): Executes a program and sends the binary output to the user.

- system(): Executes a program and gathers the output for use by PHP.

- shell_exec(): Executes a command via a shell and gathers its output for use by PHP.

- Backtick operator (for example, `command`): Identical to shell_ exec() earlier.

- pcntl_exe(): Executes a program in the current process space; that is, stops the current PHP script and replaces it with the specified program.

© Rob Aley 2016
R. Aley, *PHP CLI*, DOI 10.1007/978-1-4842-2238-6_5

- popen(): Executes a program and opens a file pointer (identical to the pointers returned by fopen(), for example) to read or write to the process via STDOUT or STDIN. Can only read or write, not both.

- proc_open(): Like popen(), but with more control. Allows both reading and writing at the same time. Not as simple to use as popen().

Which method you choose depends on what you intend to do with the newly opened process and how (or indeed if) you want to talk to it. If you're not sure from the earlier descriptions which function is appropriate for your use, the "Further Reading" list gives some pointers, information, and examples of implementations that should give you some direction.

Further Reading

- "Cookbook" recipes for using the functions listed earlier

  - http://pleac.sourceforge.net/pleac_php/
    processmanagementetc.html

- "Proc_Open: Communicate with the Outside World" tutorial by Timothy Boronczyk

  - http://www.sitepoint.com/proc-open-communicate-
    with-the-outside-world/

- "Shelling Out Sucks" by Stefan Karpinski, an article on the downsides of calling external programs via an intermediate shell

  - http://julialang.org/blog/2012/03/shelling-out-
    sucks

When calling external scripts, remember that using untrusted user input in command names or options is a recipe for bad security! The escapeshellarg() function can protect you from some inadvertent mistakes but won't stop you from executing "bad" functions or files.

Further Reading

- Sanitizing shell arguments using escapeshellarg() in the PHP manual

  - http://www.php.net/escapeshellarg

File Status and Realpath Caches

On the Web, speed is king. PHP operates two information caches to speed up access to the file system. The first is the file status cache, which caches information about a given file (such as whether it exists, whether it is readable, its size and type, and so on).

The second is the realpath cache, which caches the actual, real path for a given file or directory (expanding symlinks, relative paths, . and .. paths, include_paths and so on). Information is added to the cache automatically by PHP each time it encounters a new file and is then used by any number of functions the next time they attempt to look at that same file. With a web page that's gone in the blink of an eye where little may have happened on the file system, this is often a good trade-off for increased performance.

However, the chances that the details of a file or path may change while your script runs obviously increase with the length of time that your script takes to execute. Therefore, PHP gives you a couple of options for working with these two caches.

The following example shows the file status cache in action and how to use clearstatcache() to clear it:

```php
<?php

# Create a file and add some text to it

$filename = 'test.txt';

$handle = fopen($filename, 'w+');

fwrite($handle, 'test');

# The following should print 4

echo stat($filename)["size"]."\n";

# Now write some data to the file, increasing the file size.

fwrite($handle, 'more test');

# Intuitively, the following command should print 13 as the file is now
# bigger than before. However it still prints 4, because the filesize
# value for this file is now cached.

echo stat($filename)["size"]."\n";

# If we clear the cache ....

clearstatcache();

# then the next line should print 13 as expected

echo stat($filename)["size"]."\n";

fclose($handle);
```

The realpath cache operates in a similar way and can be cleared by calling clearstatcache(true), in other words, by calling it with true as the first parameter. You can also clear the cache for just one particular file by calling clearstatcache(true, 'myfile.txt'), where the second parameter is the file name (the first must be set to true; that is, you must also clear the realpath cache).

Of course, clearing these caches may not be necessary in your application, and doing so has performance implications. Consider each file access on a case-by-case basis.

APC and Other Code Caches

You may be aware of the APC caching system and other code caching systems that act to speed up the startup time of your script. APC, and most other systems, will not work with CLI scripts (or at least not add any benefit) because they work on a shared process model found with web servers such as Apache. PHP CLI scripts (typically) terminate their own process when they complete, so they will not work.

CHAPTER 6

■ ■ ■

Where to Now? (Or, Thanks and Feedback)

If you've read this far, thank you. I sincerely hope that this book has held your interest and has at the least informed some areas of your future PHP programming. If it has, I encourage you to start some coding right now based on one or more topics in this book while they are still fresh in your mind. People far smarter than me have shown that the sooner relevant activity occurs after learning, the easier it is to retain information and techniques over the longer term. If you use any of the techniques presented in the book in "real life," I would be interested to know! Finally, if you haven't already headed for the keyboard, don't forget to glance through the appendixes that follow. There may be something interesting or useful in there for you (either to use now or to be aware of for the future).

Giving Feedback and Getting Help and Support

E-mail: author@active-net.co.uk

Your feedback on this book, good or bad, fundamental or trivial, is solicited and welcomed. Tell me what you thought about the book, overall or a particular section. Let me know if any areas weren't covered in enough depth (or in too much detail), if any topics you were expecting weren't present, or if any of the information wasn't clear. Likewise, if you have any problems getting the sample code to run or any issues implementing the techniques discussed, please drop me a line and I'll see if there is any way I can help.

© Rob Aley 2016
R. Aley, *PHP CLI*, DOI 10.1007/978-1-4842-2238-6_6

■ ■ ■

Compiling and Installing PHP, Extensions, and Libs

There are a dozen different ways to get PHP, including downloading and compiling it yourself, downloading precompiled binaries, using package managers and software repositories, and finding it pre-installed by a forward-thinking administrator. On most Linux distributions, PHP can be installed with a one-line command such as `sudo apt-get install php5` or through graphical package managers such as the Synaptic Package Manager or the Ubuntu Software Center. Many common PHP extensions and add-ons are likewise available as prebuilt packages or alternatively through the PECL and PEAR systems.

However, sometimes it becomes necessary to do a little more work to install PHP, such as the following:

- When your project has requirements for a specific version of PHP that is different from the one shipped with your OS

- Where you need extensions not available as packages

- When you want to compile a customized version of PHP specific to your needs

Like anything involved in computers and software development, compiling PHP can take you down a rabbit hole of options, customizations, compatibility issues, libraries, and dependencies. A whole book could be written about the different possibilities (and possible headaches) involved. Luckily for us, in most use cases, the basics of compiling a standard version are quite straightforward. And like most things in life, it gets easier once you have done it once. The following section will go over the steps necessary for getting, compiling, and installing PHP and its core extensions. PHP is written in C, and because you might not be familiar with the process of compiling C programs, I have tried to explain each step to give you an idea of what is happening. This makes the process seem a little more verbose, but in reality it is quite straightforward. Go ahead and try it if you don't believe me! The next sections are also worth a read; they cover installing extras such as libraries and extensions from the PECL, PEAR, and Packagist repositories.

© Rob Aley 2016
R. Aley, *PHP CLI*, DOI 10.1007/978-1-4842-2238-6

Compiling and Installing PHP

The process for compiling and installing PHP itself varies depending on the operating system you are deploying to. The following sections deal with the main OSes that PHP is available on.

Windows

The steps outlined in the following sections are for Linux/Unix systems and use free compiler tools almost always included with the OS. For Windows, the proprietary Visual Studio compiler is required, and the steps are somewhat different (and more complicated) and thus beyond the scope of this book. You can find Windows source code, prebuilt binaries, and instructions for compiling at `http://windows.php.net/download/`, with older versions in the archive at `http://windows.php.net/downloads/releases/archives/`.

OS X

One of the easiest ways to get different versions of PHP on your Mac is by using the Macports software repository. There are currently more than 700 PHP "portfiles" covering various versions of PHP, extensions, applications, and related tools.

Toolbox	Macports
An easy-to-use system for compiling, installing, and upgrading open source software on OS X	
Main website	`https://www.macports.org/`
Installation information and documentation	`https://www.macports.org/install.php`
Directory of software available (click "php" for relevant software)	`https://www.macports.org/ports.php`

PHP also comes installed by default with recent OS X versions, although it's not always up-to-date.

If you need to compile from scratch, you can follow these steps for Linux/Unix systems. There are some issues you may run into depending on the version of OS X you are using and the version of PHP you are trying to compile. The following are the two main issues that may trip you up:

- *File/dependency locations*: These are sometimes different on OS X and may vary between versions. Where possible, always try to explicitly specify the full location path for dependencies and installation.

- *Dependency versions*: The default versions of libraries that come with OS X that core PHP and various extensions require aren't always in step with those that various versions of PHP require. Check any error messages produced during compilation (usually the first error message) for any hints as to version requirements, or check the documentation for PHP or the extension in question. Then check the documentation for the dependency to see whether it can be safely upgraded/downgraded or whether you need to install another version in parallel.

Linux/Unix

Many *nix-based operating systems have package repositories containing not just the current version of PHP but often older versions (albeit usually just the major versions). Third-party repositories can also sometimes offer an easier route to getting particular versions or configurations. So, check these out before starting to compile things yourself.

On *nix machines, the first step is to download the PHP source code from the PHP website at http://www.php.net/downloads.php. This page lists the current stable release and the previous supported stable release. Newer versions that are still under development are available at http://snaps.php.net/, and older end-of-life versions are available at http://museum.php.net/. Git users can also pull the source code down from the official mirror at https://github.com/php.

When you have identified which version you want, make a note of the URL of the .tar.gz source code file that you will use later.

```
~$ mkdir php5.4
~$ cd php5.4
~$ wget http://uk3.php.net/get/php-5.4.6.tar.gz/from/uk.php.net/mirror -o
php-5.4.6.tar.gz
~$ tar zxvf php-5.4.6.tar.gz
~$ cd php-5.4.6
```

The first two lines create a directory for your work and step into it. The directory holds the source code and intermediate files and can be deleted once PHP is installed if you want. However, it is often a good idea to keep it in case you need/want to re-install or check what version of the file you downloaded later. The third line downloads a copy of the source code file into your directory. Change the URL in the third line to that of the .tar.gz file you want to use, and change the -o option to the name of the file (otherwise, in the previous example, wget will simply call your file mirror). The fifth line unpacks the archive into a directory containing the individual source code files and changes the name of the file to the one you used on line 3. Finally, the last line steps you into the source code directory. Now you start the actual compilation process.

```
~$ ./configure
```

The `configure` command creates the "setup" for compilation. You use it to provide the settings and arguments you want for your compilation session. For instance, you can specify which core extensions you want to include in your build. If you don't specify any arguments as earlier, the defaults provided by the PHP dev team are used. This is a good choice if you don't have any particular needs and want a version that is fairly similar/compatible with the versions included with most distributions. You can also install extensions at a later date either individually or by recompiling PHP from scratch, which I will discuss in the next section. If you want to include an extension at this stage that's not included in the default settings, then this is the place to do it. For example, if you wanted to include the ldap extension, then you would change the previous command to `./configure --with-ldap[=DIR]`, where `[=DIR]` is the base installation directory of ldap on your system. You can find the exact option to use and any necessary dependencies in the PHP manual, under the "Installing/Configuring" section for the extension in question. For example, you can find details for the ldap extension at `http://www.php.net/manual/en/ldap.setup.php`. You can find a (slightly out-of-date) list of options that you can pass to the `configure` command at `http://www.php.net/manual/en/configure.about.php`; for a full list of those supported on your system in the current version you are trying to compile, you can issue the command `autoconf` followed by `./configure --help`. You can find more information about the `configure` command at `http://www.airs.com/ian/configure/`. Now you will actually compile PHP.

```
~$ make clean
~$ make
~$ sudo make install
```

You compile the binary PHP files using the make tool. The first line removes any previously created files and resets you to the start of the make process. This is not strictly necessary on your first run at compiling, but it can help if your attempt fails for some reason (such as missing dependencies, incorrect settings, unintended interruptions to the process, and so on), so including it by default is often a good choice. The second line does the actual building and compiling of the files. The third line then takes those files and installs them on the system. By default, PHP will usually be installed in the /usr/bin directory on Linux. However, you can choose where to install it by specifying a `prefix` directory at the `./configure` stage. Simply add the switch `--prefix=/path/to/dir`, where /path/to/dir is the directory into which you want PHP to be installed. This is often useful if you want to install multiple versions on the same machine (although be aware that there are other considerations when doing so). Note that the `make install` line must be run with higher permissions (`sudo`) to allow it to copy files into "privileged" locations.

If all goes well, congratulations! You have installed PHP. To check that the correct version is installed and available, use `php -v` at the command line and PHP will display the current version number. If you have installed PHP in a location outside of your search path, you will need to specify the full path name, as in `/path/to/dir/php -v`. To check which extensions and other options were installed, use `php -i` at the command line to run the `phpinfo()` function. As well as extension information (and a lot more besides), this returns a list of the options used with the `./configure` command. This can be useful when re-installing PHP or when trying to clone an installation on another machine (where the same binaries cannot just be reused).

If all doesn't go well, take a close look at the errors produced. The most common type of errors happen when your system doesn't have the relevant dependencies installed for a particular extension. Often the error message will say this explicitly, but even if it just gives you an obscure error message mentioning the name of an extension, the best advice is to double-check the installation section for that extension in the PHP manual to find out exactly what dependencies are required. Missing dependencies can often be installed using your systems package manager rather than having to manually compile them. You should also check that you have provided the location of any dependencies at the configure stage if required.

If all else fails, copy and paste the exact error message into your favorite Internet search engine, probably starting with the first error message shown if multiple errors appear. Many people have compiled PHP, and most errors have been encountered and documented online. Don't let all this talk of errors put you off trying to compile PHP. Errors are more likely to occur the more complicated you make your configuration, and if you're careful about dependencies, you can often avoid them altogether. So, first try a straightforward compilation with the default options to get the hang of things and then take it from there!

You can find more information on installations, with a general focus on web servers but otherwise useful, in the PHP manual at http://www.php.net/manual/en/install.php.

Compiling and Installing (Extra) Core Extensions

As you saw in the previous section, the most common way to install core extensions is to enable the relevant flags at the configure stage during compilation of the main PHP installation (note, by default, many extensions are automatically enabled). However, it's not uncommon to come across the need to install an additional extension later, for instance, as the requirements for your program change from its initial design. There are two ways to approach this. The first, which you'll find recommended a lot online, is to redo the compilation/installation of PHP from scratch, adding the newly required modules at the configure stage (after issuing php -i to remember what configure options you used the first time). While this works perfectly well, compiling the full PHP binaries is a bit of a slog, which can take older PCs in particular a long time to complete. There is a shortcut, however.

Each of the core extensions is actually a separate .so binary and can be compiled independently. To do this, follow the first steps in the previous section to download and unpack the PHP source code and step into the directory. If you haven't deleted it from when you compiled PHP, it should be ready to go. Within the source code is a directory called ext, inside of which are separate directories for each of the extensions.

```
~$ cd ext
~$ ls
```

This will show you all the core extensions available. For instance, if you want to add the pcntl extension (used in this book for daemon software), you can enter the pnctl directory and compile/install just that extension in a similar manner to how you compiled the whole PHP package in the previous section.

```
~$ cd pcntl
~$ phpize
~$ ./configure
~$ make clean
~$ make
~$ sudo make install
```

The additional command, phpize, is used to prepare the build environment for the extension. This is not necessary when building the full PHP binaries, but it is when building individual extensions. If you find that you don't have phpize on your system, it is often available through your system's package manager in the php-dev package (for example, on Ubuntu, it is available as phpize5 in the php5-dev package). You can find more details about phpize and getting it at http://us.php.net/manual/en/install. pecl.phpize.php.

Once you have run the previous commands, you should find that a .so file (pcntl. so in this example) has been compiled and placed in PHP's extension directory. The final step is to tell PHP about it by adding the following line somewhere in your php.ini file:

```
extension=pcntl.so
```

If you're not sure where your php.ini file is, you can run php -i | grep "Loaded Configuration File" on the command line to find out. You can also use php -i to check that your extension is now correctly installed and available for use.

Installing Multiple Versions of PHP

Sometimes (particularly on development machines) you may want to install multiple versions of PHP at the same time, for instance, if you are deploying to end users with PHP already installed but who may have different versions. One straightforward way to achieve this is to create a set of virtual machines (I use VirtualBox for this) with a different version of PHP installed in each. In this scenario, you can always be sure which version you are running and that the installation and configuration of one version isn't interfering with that of another. The downside is that it can be slow to start up and shut down different VMs (or a hit on resources to run them all at once), and if you are using proprietary OSs like Windows, you can incur additional licensing costs. It is possible to have multiple versions installed and running directly on the same machine; however, if you are not careful, it can become a nightmare trying to keep the versions and their dependencies separate and making sure you know which version you are using at all times. As such, I am not going to delve into it in this book. However, the following are two articles from respected PHP community members who have done just that, which may give you some pointers on what to do and the pitfalls involved. I suggest that before you try this, you become intimately familiar with compiling and installing PHP, the file and directory structures and locations that PHP uses, and how to check which versions of PHP and extensions are running.

There are also a couple of relevant tools listed here. The first is php-build, which automatically builds multiple versions of PHP from source, although you still need to exercise care installing and using them simultaneously. The second is 3v4l.org, a web service that allows you to test chunks of code in 90+ versions of PHP at the same time. This may avoid the need for installing multiple versions at all. And the final tool is a library that simulates many functions from newer versions for use with older versions.

Further Reading

- Installing multiple versions, using SVN

    - `http://derickrethans.nl/multiple-php-version-setup.html`

- Installing multiple versions, using GIT

    - `http://mark-story.com/posts/view/installing-multiple-versions-of-php-from-source`

Toolbox	php-build

php-build automatically builds multiple PHP versions from source that can be used in parallel.

Main website	`https://php-build.github.io/`

Toolbox	3v4l.org

Web service that allows you test chunks of code in 90+ versions of PHP with the click of one button

Main website	`http://3v4l.org`

Toolbox	upgrade.php

Library to emulate newer functions for older versions of PHP

Main website	`http://include-once.org/p/upgradephp/`

PEAR and PECL

PHP Extension and Application Repository (PEAR) is a library of code and extensions written in PHP, with an easy-to-use packaging and distribution system. PHP Extension Community Library (PECL) is essentially the same but is for extensions written in C.

Both PECL and PEAR work in a similar way to package managers such as Debians apt-get. For example, to install the Cairo graphics extension from PECL, simply use `sudo pecl install cairo` at the command line. This will download, compile, and install Cairo for you, and you can then start using it from within your PHP scripts. Similarly, to install the RDF extension from PEAR, use `pear install rdf`.

The pear and `pecl` commands are included as standard with PHP; however, some package managers put them in the optional php-dev or php-pear package. On Ubuntu, for instance, use `sudo apt-get install php-pear` to install it.

You can find more information on both tools as well as the hundreds of extensions and libraries available, at `http://pear.php.net` and `http://pecl.php.net`, respectively.

Composer

Composer is a dependency manager. While it deals with packages, it is not a package manager like PEAR. Rather than installing packages centrally, it deals with them on a per-project basis, ensuring that the appropriate versions of the relevant packages, and their dependencies, are installed automatically for that project.

The basic Composer workflow happens as follows:

1. You install Composer.

2. In the base directory of your project, you create a JSON-formatted file called `composer.json` that specifies which packages (and versions) your project needs.

3. In that directory, you run Composer. It will fetch and install all of the specified packages and will automatically also install any of the other packages that those you have specified depend on (and so on until all dependencies are satisfied).

4. In your PHP code, simply add the function `require 'vendor/autoload.php';` and your libraries will be automatically available when you use them.

Fully comprehensive documentation, aimed at beginners as well as advanced users, is available on the Composer website. Composer itself doesn't host any packages; that is the job of package repositories. Packagist is the main, and currently the only, comprehensive public repository, and it is the default used by Composer. You can browse the thousands of available packages on the Packagist website. You can, of course, specify a different repository and indeed create and use your own packages privately if you need.

Toolbox	Composer Dependency Manager
The easy way to keep libraries consistent and up-to-date on a per-project basis	
Main website	`http://getcomposer.org`
Package repository	`https://packagist.org`
Tutorial	`http://code.tutsplus.com/tutorials/easy-package-management-with-composer--net-25530`

Symfony2 Bundles

If you're using the Symfony2 framework, you can choose from and download more than 1,000 useful code bundles from knpbundles. These can be installed manually or often using the Composer dependency system (see the previous section). Visit `http://knpbundles.com/` for more information and to browse the available code.

APPENDIX B

Sources of Help

Even with excellent books like this on the market, you will sometimes need a little additional help when you come across a tricky problem with PHP. The following are some potential sources of help.

The PHP Manual

You can find the official PHP manual online at http://php.net/docs.php. The manual provides fairly comprehensive documentation in the main on PHP installation, syntax, functions, and many extensions. Of particular note are the user comments at the bottom of each page. These are generally helpful and offer real-world advice related to the function or topic of the page. Occasionally some duff advice is given in the comments; however, this is usually corrected or mentioned in a subsequent comment, so it's worth reading through all the comments on a given page.

A handy function of the online manual is that you can do a quick lookup of a function or topic by typing it as the first part of a URL. For instance, if you can't remember what the parameters of strripos() are, you can simply type http://php.net/strripos into your browser and you will be sent straight to the relevant page. Likewise, if you want a quick refresher on how PHP handles arrays, visit http://php.net/array and you'll go straight to the array page in the language/types section of the manual.

If you don't always have an Internet connection, you can also download a copy of the manual from http://www.php.net/download-docs.php. It is available as HTML, as Unix-style man pages, and in Microsoft Compiled HTML Manual (CHM) format.

Official Mailing Lists

There are a number of official mailing lists at http://php.net/mailing-lists.php covering a wide variety of topics. Of note for getting help are the "General user list" for general queries and the "Windows PHP users list" for Windows-specific questions. Beware when subscribing that some of the lists are quite busy and you will get a large number of e-mails each day. The archives are available online if you just want to browse them or get a feel for the volume generated on each list.

© Rob Aley 2016
R. Aley, *PHP CLI*, DOI 10.1007/978-1-4842-2238-6

Stack Overflow

If you're not familiar with it, Stack Overflow (http://stackoverflow.com) is a prolific "question and answer" site aimed at programmers. Unlike some Q&A sites, you don't need to join or pay to view the answers to questions, ads are limited, and there are millions of answered questions on the site. This includes a good chunk of PHP-related questions.

All questions and answers are "tagged" with their topics so that you can find the ones relevant to you. To browse questions tagged with PHP, visit http://stackoverflow.com/questions/tagged/php. You can also use the site's search facility; to narrow your search to only PHP-related answers, add "[tag]" to your search. For example, if you want to search for questions about the date function, which is a common word in English and a common function name in many programming languages, search for "[php] date" to get only PHP-specific information.

At the time of writing, there were 942,629 questions tagged with "php," 1,126 tagged with "php" *and* "command-line," and 1,172 tagged with "php" *and* "cli." The moderators are usually very quick at shutting down duplicate questions, so you can see from these numbers that a lot of relevant information is available.

Other Books

While you may think that this is the only book on PHP you will ever need, I have been told that there may be other PHP books available. While I can't recommend any specifically (other than those I have already noted in the relevant chapters), if you browse any big-name bookseller, you will find a plethora of PHP-related titles. And of course you can browse the 70+ PHP-related books by my esteemed publisher at http://www.apress.com/programming/php.

Newsgroups

PHP has a set of official newsgroups listed and archived at http://news.php.net/ that cover a wide range of PHP topic areas. These may be worth a browse and sometimes can elicit a response to queries (although some of the internals lists are definitely not for the faint-hearted).

PHP Subredit

The PHP "subreddit" on Reddit.com at http://www.reddit.com/r/PHP/ is a mixture of PHP news, opinions, useful links, and requests for help. Although usually genuinely interesting with helpful responses to questions, an occasional assortment of trolls and unhelpful/rude people can be found here as well. A more tolerant subreddit for getting help is "phphelp" at https://www.reddit.com/r/phphelp, which was specifically set up to answer questions (even from beginners).

PHP on GitHub

Sometimes the best way to solve a problem is to look at similar code other people have written. GitHub, the popular source repository website, has tons of the stuff to plow through. You can search all the code repositories at `https://github.com/search`, and you can use the modifier "language:php" in your search terms to narrow your results to projects using your favorite language. If you just want to keep an eye on what PHP projects are popular these days, you can check out the PHP trending list at `https://github.com/trending?l=php`.

PHP News Sites

Although not usually good for direct help, PHP news sites and mailing lists can keep you up-to-date with essentials such as security alerts, useful and interesting articles, and announcements of new projects, libraries, and tutorials that you may not even know you needed yet! Some of the more popular ones are listed here:

PHPDeveloper: `http://phpdeveloper.org/`
Planet PHP: `http://www.planet-php.net/`
PHP Weekly News: `http://www.phpweekly.com/`
PHPBuilder: `http://www.phpbuilder.com/`

Index

A, B

APC caching system, 44

C

CLI programming
  CLI SAPI, 8
  coding frameworks, 12
  compromised files, 11
  HTTP, 7
  performance, 9
  PHP programmers, 7
  source code, 10
  users misbehaving, 11
CLI SAPIc
  command-line
    arguments, 20–21
  constants/variables, 29
  EIM, 16, 24
  exit code, 26
  HTML version, 18
  installation, 14
  IPv6, 16
  PATHEXT environment, 25
  PHP, 13
  PHP binary, 15
  PHP code, 21
  php-win.exe, 25
  reflection, 19
  REPL, 27
  scripts, 5
  STDIN, 22
  string, 22
  syntax errors, 16
  Unix/Linux systems, 23
  and web implementation, 13

Compiling and installing PHP
  core extensions, 51
  error message, 51
  OS X, 48
  PHP files, 50
  versions, 52
  Windows, 48
Composer, 54
Composer dependency system, 55

D

Dependency versions, 49

E, F

Extended Information Mode (EIM), 16, 24

G

GitHub, 59
Graphical user interface (GUI)
  applications, 4, 38

H

HTTP headers, 7, 13

I, J, K

Integrated development environments
  (IDEs), 17–18

L, M, N

Laravel Framework Artisan Console tool, 40
Linux/Unix, 49

© Rob Aley 2016
R. Aley, *PHP CLI*, DOI 10.1007/978-1-4842-2238-6

■ O

Official mailing lists, 57
Official newsgroups, 58
Online manual, 57
Operating systems, 3

■ P, Q

PHP
    advantage, 2
    CLI scripts, 5
    CLI software, 2
    external tools, 4
    operating systems, 3
    programming
        concepts, 3
php-build, 52
PHP CLI scripts
    APC caching system, 44
    benefits, 41
    external scripts, 42
    file status and Realpath
        caches, 42
PHP Extension and Application
    Repository (PEAR), 53
PHP Extension Community Library
    (PECL), 53
PHP manual, 57
PHP news sites, 59
PHP programming, 45
PHP REPL, 27
PHP Subredit, 58
php-win.exe, 25
POSIX-compliant
    operating system, 3

■ R

Realpath cache, 44
REPL session, 27

■ S, T

Shelling out, 41
Software security, 10
Source code, 10
Stack overflow, 58
Symfony2 framework, 55
Symfony console component, 40
Synaptic Package Manager, 47

■ U

Ubuntu Software Center, 47
upgrade.php, 53
User-facing software
    advanced command-line input, 35, 37
    command-line interface basics, 31–32
    keyboard input, 35
    libraries/components, 40
    outputting text, 35
    PHP CLI SAPI, 38
    program flow control, 35
    STDOUT, 40

■ V

3v4l.org, 53

■ W, X, Y, Z

Webmozart Console toolkit, 40

Get the eBook for only $5!

Why limit yourself?

Now you can take the weightless companion with you wherever you go and access your content on your PC, phone, tablet, or reader.

Since you've purchased this print book, we're happy to offer you the eBook in all 3 formats for just $5.

Convenient and fully searchable, the PDF version enables you to easily find and copy code—or perform examples by quickly toggling between instructions and applications. The MOBI format is ideal for your Kindle, while the ePUB can be utilized on a variety of mobile devices.

To learn more, go to www.apress.com/companion or contact support@apress.com.

All Apress eBooks are subject to copyright. All rights are reserved by the Publisher, whether the whole or part of the material is concerned, specifically the rights of translation, reprinting, reuse of illustrations, recitation, broadcasting, reproduction on microfilms or in any other physical way, and transmission or information storage and retrieval, electronic adaptation, computer software, or by similar or dissimilar methodology now known or hereafter developed. Exempted from this legal reservation are brief excerpts in connection with reviews or scholarly analysis or material supplied specifically for the purpose of being entered and executed on a computer system, for exclusive use by the purchaser of the work. Duplication of this publication or parts thereof is permitted only under the provisions of the Copyright Law of the Publisher's location, in its current version, and permission for use must always be obtained from Springer. Permissions for use may be obtained through RightsLink at the Copyright Clearance Center. Violations are liable to prosecution under the respective Copyright Law.

Printed in the United States
By Bookmasters